Gnostic Celtic Church
A Manual and Book of Liturgy

Compiled and Edited by
John Michael Greer

The Gnostic Celtic Church:

A Manual and Book of Liturgy

Compiled and Edited by John Michael Greer

ISBN: 978-1-939790-05-7

Greer, John Michael
The Gnostic Celtic Church:
A Manual and Book of Liturgy/John Michael Greer

First Edition: April 2013

Printed in the United States of America

9 8 7 6 5 4 3 2 1 0

Starseed Publications
2204 E Grand Ave.
Everett, WA 98201

Contents

Introduction

I have long thought that the independent sacramental movement ranks among the most promising stars now rising above the horizon of contemporary spirituality. That diverse body of monastics and mystics, bishops, priests, priestesses, and laypeople who have embraced the inner experiential heritage of Western sacramental religion, while rejecting its dogmatic and authoritarian perversions, has as yet barely registered on the fringes of the collective conversation of our time. Still, some of the most thoughtful and innovative work in today's religious scene is taking shape in the independent churches and religious orders of that movement.

When I became the seventh Grand Archdruid of the Ancient Order of Druids in America (AODA) in 2003, the thought of participating in that movement in any active role was nowhere in my mind. My hope was simply to help revive a Druid order that was at that time on the brink of extinction. Only when the initial hard work of relaunching the order and revising its rituals and teachings was past did I begin to get some idea of just how much of the last century or so of alternative spirituality in America and elsewhere had helped shape the traditions AODA's elderly members handed down to me. The teachings and documents I received then and later, and the initiations and consecrations that came with them, included material and lineages from several branches of the independent sacramental movement. That heritage cried out for exploration and inclusion in the AODA tradition; one result, more than a decade later, is this book.

I owe a great deal to the people who made this portion of my own spiritual journey possible. Foremost among them is Dr. John Gilbert, who introduced me to the AODA as well as the Universal Gnostic tradition, helped me make sense of the connections between them, and was the principal consecrator at my episcopal consecration in 2004. Special thanks are also owed to Bishop John Plummer, who consecrated me *sub conditione* in 2007 and communicated to me several other lineages and empowerments at the same time, and taught me a great deal about the potentials for diversity and creativity within a tradition that I, raised outside Christianity, had always understood in far too narrow a sense.

The other current archdruids of AODA, Sara Greer, Gordon Cooper, and Siani Overstreet, all willingly contributed to the complex process of enriching contemporary Druidry with a modern nature-centered Gnosticism. Here as so often, though, my deepest thanks are owed to the members of AODA, whose enthusiasm for a spirituality that pays little heed to conventional notions about religion and the inner life continues to startle and inspire me.

/I\ John Michael Greer
Presiding Archbishop, GCC
Spring Equinox 2013

The Gnostic Celtic Church

The Gnostic Celtic Church (GCC) is an independent sacramental church of nature spirituality affiliated with the Ancient Order of Druids in America (AODA), a contemporary Druid order. Like many other alternative spiritual groups in American society, AODA—which was originally founded in 1912—developed connections with a variety of other compatible traditions over the course of its history. One of these connections was with the Universal Gnostic Church (UGC).

After the revival of AODA began in 2003, its archdruids and members began to discuss the possibility and value of a branch of the UGC tradition specifically oriented to AODA's system of nature spirituality and contemporary Druid teachings. After much discussion and reflection, the GCC was accordingly founded on December 22, 2010, as part of a general reorganization of AODA's activities.

The GCC now functions as the center of the religious dimension of the AODA tradition, and is responsible for the education and ordination of Druid clergy in AODA. What sets it apart from most alternative religious groups nowadays is that the GCC does not train people for the standard American Protestant model of the clergy—a model that assigns to clergy the functions of providing weekly services to a congregation, "marrying and burying," offering amateur counseling to parishioners, and pursuing political and social causes of one kind or another, and defines training for the ministry in terms of the same style of university education used by most other service professions.

This model evolved out of the distinctive social and theological requirements of American Protestant Christianity and has little relevance to other faiths, especially those that do not have the financial resources to support full-time ministers. It has nonetheless been adopted uncritically by a great many alternative religious traditions here in America. It was in response to the very poor fit between that model and the needs of a contemporary alternative religious movement that AODA chose to pursue an older model better suited to its own tradition and needs.

The GCC thus has chosen to establish what was once called a regular clergy, as distinct from a secular clergy—that is to say, something much closer to monks than to ministers. This was the core model for clergy in the old Celtic Church in Ireland, Wales, Brittany, and other Celtic nations, in the days before the Roman papacy imposed its rule on the lands of Europe's far west. Members of the Celtic clergy were monks first and foremost, living lives focused on service to the Divine rather than the needs of a congregation, and those who functioned as priests for local communities did so as a small portion of a monastic lifestyle that embraced many other dimensions.

It has been suggested by scholars that the Celtic church's monastic model of priesthood may well have been influenced by the traditions of the ancient Druids, who were still a living presence in Ireland, Wales, and elsewhere in the Celtic world at the time the Celtic Church first emerged there. Whether or not this is the case, that model is far more relevant to the modern Druid tradition than is the Protestant Christian model copied by so many alternative faiths nowadays.

The specific rules and disciplines of Christian monasticism are not relevant to a modern Druid tradition, to be sure, and a case could be made that many of them are no longer relevant to the modern world more generally. Still, there is certainly a need for men and women who are willing to embrace a new monasticism centered on a personal rule: one in which the core principle of aligning the whole life with the spiritual dimensions of reality can express itself in forms relevant to the individual practitioner and the present age, in which a rich spiritual life supported by meaningful ceremonial and personal practice can readily coexist with whatever form of outward life is necessary or appropriate to each priest or priestess, and in which the practice of sacramental spirituality can be pursued apart from the various pathologies of political religion.

This concept, which the GCC terms "the Hermitage of the Heart," is what the GCC offers to those members of AODA who are interested in following the path of a priest or priestess. It is obviously not for everyone, but it is our belief and hope that many will find the path of the Gnostic Celtic Church relevant to their own lives.

Sources of the GCC

The Universal Gnostic Church was founded in 1952 by Revs. Omar Zasluchy, Owen Symanski, and Matthew Shaw, three dissident ministers of the Universalist Church. Little remembered nowadays except by historians of liberal religion and by the Unitarian Church, which absorbed it via a merger in 1961, the Universalist Church was a significant presence in 19th and early 20th century American religion, with hundreds of congregations across the country and a lively literature. Its distinctive (and, at the time, highly controversial) doctrine was the insistence that all souls, without exception, must attain salvation; the notion that any soul whatsoever could be condemned to eternal damnation was in the Universalist view incompatible with faith in a loving and merciful God.

The reasons that led the three founders of the UGC to break from the Universalist Church and found their own church are not described in the very limited documentation that survives from the UGC's origin. The first steps toward union with the Unitarian Church, which were taken around that time, likely had much to do with the matter. The Unitarian Church's movement toward an essentially agnostic stance on most religious subjects over the course of the twentieth century was a source of difficulty for many Universalists during the debate on uniting the two denominations. While the union did finally take place in 1961, not all Universalist clergy or laypeople went with their church into the new, combined Unitarian Universalist denomination. The UGC was created by one small subset of those who did not.

In its first days, the Universal Gnostic Church called its presiding ministers apostles. At some point during the 1950s or 1960s, according to oral accounts by later bishops of the church, the three founding apostles apparently received consecration and apostolic succession from a bishop in one of the French Gnostic lineages, and thereafter used the title of bishop in place of apostle. Our research has not been able to trace the details of the lineage that was received at that time, and its exact nature and antecedents remain an open question. As mentioned further on in this essay, UGC bishops later obtained reconsecration from a different source to secure a fully traceable lineage of apostolic succession.

The fusion of Universalism with the teachings of the French Gnostic Revival made for an unusual approach to most religious questions, one that veered well outside the territory of the religious mainstream of the time. The unconventional nature of the UGC and its teachings were considerably amplified, though, when Bishop (and former Apostle) Matthew Shaw, one of the three founders of the UGC, came into contact with Dr. Juliet Ashley, at that time Grand Archdruid of the Ancient Order of Druids in America. Ashley was an American occultist of what used to be the classic type, a gifted folk healer, hypnotist and therapist as well as an initiate in a number of esoteric lineages.

Sometime after 1972, when he moved to Boulder, Colorado, Shaw became a member of AODA and most of the other orders headed by Ashley. In 1978, in turn, Ashley resigned her position in AODA and Shaw, taking the religious name Rhodonn Starrus, became the fourth Grand Archdruid of that order. From this time on, all of the archdruids of the order have been consecrated ex officio as Gnostic bishops in the UGC lineage. That heritage was passed in turn to the current Grand Archdruid of AODA, John Michael Greer, who was consecrated in 2004, and to the other current archdruids, who were consecrated by Greer and others in the years immediately thereafter. It was on this foundation that the Gnostic Celtic Church was established in 2010.

Teachings of the GCC

The Gnostic Celtic Church draws its teachings from a medley of influences including the Druid Revival, the Gnostic revival, the old Universalist Church, and the independent sacramental movement. While no attempt is made to dogmatize—in this, as in all Gnostic traditions, personal religious experience is the goal that is set before each aspirant and the sole basis on which questions of a religious nature can be answered—certain teachings have been embraced as the core values from which the GCC as an organization derives its broad approach to spiritual issues. Those core teachings may be summarized in the words "Gnostic, Universalist, and Pelagian."

Gnostic

The word Gnostic comes from the Greek word gnosis, which means "personal knowledge" or "recognition." The term was used as a self-description by a diverse and highly creative religious movement that began around the start of the Christian era and continued for several centuries before it was obliterated by religious persecution. Beginning in the 19th century, in an interesting parallel with the 18th century revival of Druidry, the fragments of ancient Gnostic teachings helped spark a series of modern movements that borrowed the concept of gnosis and the ancient Gnostic teaching that personal experience, rather than dogmatic belief or membership in an organization, can form the heart of a spiritual path. As part of the modern Gnostic movement, the GCC affirms that individual experience is central to its own vision of spirituality.

Universalist

Some of the ancient Gnostics, like the mainstream religious movements that persecuted and eventually destroyed them, taught that certain people were capable of reaching the goals of the spiritual path but others were doomed to fail. An alternative view, taught by the great mystic Origen among others, held that communion with spiritual realities is open to every being without exception, and that all beings—again, without exception—will eventually enter into harmony with the Divine. This belief may be found in many alternative spiritual traditions in the West; it has been central to the contemporary Druid movement since the early days of the Druid Revival; and it became the foundation of the Universalist heresy, and later of the Universalist Church. As one heir of their legacy, the GCC affirms that the recognition of the potential for

7

spiritual achievement in all beings is central to its own vision of spirituality.

Pelagian

Pelagius was a Christian mystic who was born in Wales in the 4th century, was ordained in the Celtic Church, and taught what later came to be called the Pelagian heresy—the teaching that the salvation of each individual is entirely the result of that individual's own efforts, and can neither be gained through anyone else's merits or denied on account of anyone else's failings. This teaching, which contradicted orthodox doctrines of original sin and substituted atonement, nonetheless remained part of the teachings of the Celtic Church, and of many other alternative movements from the Middle Ages to the present. As an inheritor of a number of these traditions, the GCC affirms that the value of personal responsibility and personal freedom is central to its own vision of spirituality.

As befits a church founded on the principle of individual spiritual experience, the GCC does not require its members or any person whatsoever to accept any of these teachings, but it does expect its priests and priestesses to be familiar with them, to understand their meaning and value within the GCC's tradition, and to be able to discuss them intelligently.

Beyond these, and on the same terms, the GCC accepts certain basic principles that are common to most of the world's religions and spiritual paths. It accepts, for example, that the universe we see is a reflection of an invisible reality we do not normally see; that there are many other beings in the universe besides humanity, some less complex and intelligent than humanity, some more so; that each human being has a dimension that transcends the physical and is capable of surviving the death of the physical body; that the incidents of life on Earth are not merely random, but are obedient to purposes greater than those we know; and that a personal relationship based on reverence and gratitude is an appropriate way of interaction with spiritual powers and of participation in the cosmos as a whole.

It will be noticed that the GCC does not specify the number, gender, or nature of the spiritual powers its deacons, priests and priestesses, and bishops invoke. This is quite deliberate, and derives from the points already made. Human beings around the world and throughout time have encountered a rich diversity of divine beings and of impersonal spiritual powers, and have drawn inspiration, benediction, and guidance from them all. Though it is common in today's popular religious culture to insist that all this diversity must somehow be the expression of a single reality, the jury remains out on that claim, and the GCC chooses not to take a position on an issue that human beings may never be able to settle for certain.

One or many, personal or impersonal, gods or goddesses or some of each—these questions are left to the free choice and the personal experience of the individual. Still, there is one limitation, which is that the spiritual practices of the GCC presuppose a belief in, and an orientation toward, some power or powers greater than humanity, with whom a personal relationship is possible. Those who reject such a belief and orientation are entirely free to do so, in or out of AODA, but they will not benefit from the training the GCC provides for its clergy and therefore are not eligible for training and ordination. We encourage them to seek elsewhere for a system of training better suited to their needs.

Holy Orders and Apostolic Succession

The GCC confers three holy orders, or stages in priestly training and initiation, upon its clergy. Reception into the order of deacon is available to members of AODA who have been initiated into the First Degree of AODA and desire to pursue ordination to the priesthood. Ordination into the order of priest or priestess is reserved for those deacons of the GCC who have completed the study program described in a later section of this book, and have also been initiated into the Second Degree of AODA. Consecration into the order of bishop is reserved for those priests and priestesses of the GCC who have designed and completed a personal study program building on that established by the GCC for its priests and priestesses, and have

9

also been initiated into the Third Degree of AODA. Ordination is not merely a result of initiation into AODA degrees; it must be earned by work beyond that required for the degrees.

Holy orders conferred by the GCC must be earned within the GCC training program. Those individuals who have been ordained as deacons, priests or priestesses, or bishops in other churches, even if in possession of valid orders, have not received the specific training and preparation that GCC clergy are expected to have. Those who have been received, ordained, or consecrated in other lineages are certainly welcome to participate in the GCC training program, and upon completion of each level, will receive the appropriate ordination or consecration *sub conditione.**

The GCC, while it is not exclusively a Christian church, has inherited apostolic succession — the communication of lineage that reaches back from each bishop through the line of his or her consecrators to one or more of the disciples of Jesus of Nazareth — as one of the currents of energy that flow into its tradition and are communicated to its ordinands. After the passing of Matthew Shaw, John Gilbert, a bishop in the UGC as well as one of AODA's archdruids at that time, set about renewing the apostolic succession of the UGC when it became clear that the details of Shaw's consecration could not be traced. As a result, Gilbert sought and received *sub conditione* consecration from Bishop Lewis Keizer of the Church of Antioch. More recently, two of the GCC's present archbishops were also consecrated by Bishop John Plummer, an independent bishop holding many lines of succession, and have transmitted this consecration to the other GCC bishops.

Because the GCC is not exclusively a Christian church, its apostolic succession is not accepted by most Christian churches, and we recommend that those who are interested in being ordained and consecrated in a lineage of apostolic succession accepted by the bulk of sacramental Christian churches should seek it from another source. We regard apostolic succession, and confer it within our own lineage, as one of a variety of diverse currents of spiritual power that have

---

* This is a technical term for an ordination or consecration given subsequent to an existing ordination or consecration.

descended to us from the past, and that help shape our unfolding tradition of contemporary nature spirituality.

The Rule of Awen

In the monastic traditions of other faiths, a formal rule of life plays a central role in the activities of the regular clergy, and indeed the term "regular clergy" itself (which derives from the Latin word *regula*, "rule") derives from that custom. While details vary from order to order and from faith to faith, the core principle of each such rule is the whole and unreserved dedication of the self to the divine. Each precept of a monastic rule serves as a means by which the details of daily life may be brought into accordance with this central principle, and common obstacles to that reorientation of life may be avoided.

That principle, in the great majority of these faiths, finds its usual expression in terms of a highly specific rule of life in which prohibitions central to the wider faith are taken to extremes. Religious traditions that are uncomfortable with human sexuality, for example, normally expect their monks and nuns to accept a lifelong avoidance of any form of sexual contact; faiths that have a difficult relationship with the concept of individual freedom and autonomy, similarly, tend to expect vows of obedience from their regular clergy. Druidry has no such discomfort with either of these elements of life, or for that matter of anything else that is part of the way of Nature, so a rule suitable for the regular clergy of a Druid order must take a different approach.

That approach takes its beginning from one of the central concepts of the contemporary Druid movement: Awen, the spirit of inspiration. Each soul, according to the lore of the Druid Revival, has its own unique Awen. To put the same concept in terms that may be slightly more familiar to many readers, each soul has its own purpose in existence, which differs from that of every other soul, and it has the capacity—and ultimately the necessity—of coming to know, understand, and fulfill this unique purpose.

In *Barddas*, the anthology of 19th century Druid traditions compiled from the writings of seminal Druid Revival author Iolo

Morganwg, a unique Awen is said to be present in each soul from the moment it comes into being, and guides it on its long journey up through the Circle of Abred—the realm of incarnate life in all its myriad forms—to the human level of existence. It is at the human level that the individual Awen for the first time may become an object of conscious awareness. Achieving this awareness, and living in accord with it, is according to these Druid teachings the great challenge of human existence, and the degree of each life's success or failure at this task determines whether the soul proceeds into the radiant life of Gwynfydd, remains at the human level for another incarnation, or returns to some earlier point in the realm of Abred to recapitulate its journey and learn the lessons that were inadequately absorbed the first time through.

Thus the rule of life that the clergy of the Gnostic Celtic Church are asked to embrace may be defined simply by these words: *find and follow your own Awen*. Taken as seriously as it should be—for there is no greater challenge for any human being than that of seeking his or her purpose in existence, and then placing the fulfillment of that purpose above other concerns as a guide to action and life—this is as demanding a rule as the strictest of traditional monastic vows. Following it requires close attention to the highest and deepest dimensions of the inner life, and a willingness to ignore all the pressures of the ego and the world when those come into conflict, as they will, with the ripening personal knowledge of the path that Awen reveals.

It also requires, crucially, a willingness to renounce one of the less creditable dimensions of today's popular culture—the widespread conviction that having some particular set of beliefs makes one better, wiser, more honest, more realistic, more sophisticated, or more of some other praiseworthy quality than those who have different beliefs. Each person's Awen, as already noted, is unique, and a way of understanding the cosmos and the spiritual powers that shape it that is perfectly appropriate for one person will be hopelessly misguided for others. Thus a respect for individual differences in belief and practice is mandated by the Rule of Awen: those who claim the right to follow the guidance of a personal spiritual vision themselves, by that very fact, renounce the right to pass judgment on the personal spiritual vision of others.

From this recognition comes one of the few prohibitions placed on the clergy of the Gnostic Celtic Church. Receiving holy orders in the GCC is not a conferral of authority over others in matters of faith and morals, or in any other context, but an acceptance of responsibility for oneself and one's own life and work. The clergy of the GCC are encouraged to teach by example, and to offer advice and instruction in spiritual and other matters to those who may request such services, but it is no part of their duty to tell other people how to live their lives.

If, upon reflection, a candidate for holy orders comes to believe that it is essential to his or her Awen to claim religious or moral authority over others as part of the priestly role he or she seeks, he or she will be asked to seek ordination from some other source. If one who is already ordained or consecrated in the GCC comes to the same belief, in turn, it will be his or her duty—a duty that will if necessary be enforced by the Grand Grove—to leave the GCC and pursue another path.

The Hermitage of the Heart

So personal a way of life as that defined by the Rule of Awen requires a conception of the role of regular clergy that is more closely akin to that of the independent hermit than that of the monk or nun living under a collective discipline. Still, the traditional solitude of the hermit is neither easy to attain in today's crowded world nor appropriate for the needs, and the Awen, of many people otherwise well suited to the work of the GCC. In place of the outward trappings of the hermit's life, therefore, the GCC proposes an inner orientation— the Hermitage of the Heart.

The life of any person who cultivates an inner life and an orientation toward the Divine in today's obsessively materialistic world must inevitably have important resonances with the lives of hermits in other ages. There is the same sense of standing apart from the outer world, the same embrace of a freely chosen discipline, the same provision of a place of solitude; the difference is simply that the most suitable place of solitude for the hermit of today is found within his or her own heart.

The practice of the Hermitage of the Heart embraces the whole of life; it calls on the priest or priestess to maintain the inner clarity and the spiritual orientation of a hermit in a hermitage all through his or her daily round. Within that framework, the more specific practices that are recommended to the priests and priestesses of the Gnostic Celtic Church have their places: the practices of the home altar, morning prayer, and evening lection, to enrich and orient the inner life; the Communion ritual to provide the central flame around which the rest of the inner Hermitage is built; the solitary Grove ritual to provide symbolic structure to that Hermitage; and the Sphere of Protection ritual to define and maintain the boundaries of the Hermitage against the pressures of a far from supportive world.

Those who feel called to explore or embrace these possibilities are welcome to read further, and to apply for reception as deacons according to the forms and requirements outlined later in this book.

The Gnosis of Nature

The decision by the founders of the Universal Gnostic Church to take the name and embrace the heritage of the ancient Gnostics has been a source of some confusion in recent years. The Gnostic traditions of the ancient world included a vast diversity of teachings and practices, but most of those that have become famous in recent years shared the same disdain for physical existence, physical embodiment, and sexuality that pervaded so much of later Greek philosophy, and left lasting and unhelpful traces in the mainstream forms of Christianity.

Such classic Gnostic writings as *The Secret Book of John* and The *Hypostasis of the Archons* present a harshly dualist vision of reality in which the entire material world is the evil creation of a false god, and the sole hope of the human spirit is in headlong flight out of the world of matter toward a distant and disembodied realm of light. Nor is this escape available to all; in many of these ancient Gnostic texts, salvation was held to be possible only for a small minority of human beings.

The discovery of the Nag Hammadi texts in Egypt in 1945 was the event that brought this side of the Gnostic movement so forcefully into the public eye. Most of the Nag Hammadi documents, as it happened, came from the dualist end of the Gnostic movement. As a result, a great many people have come to think that Gnosticism can only be understood as a dualistic, world-hating, and elitist faith. It requires a closer look at the entire body of Gnostic literature to recognize that this was only one aspect of a much more diverse and creative movement that also included visions of reality in which the oneness of the cosmos was a central theme, and in which the body and the material world were points of access to the divine rather than obstacles to its manifestation.

The revival of Gnostic spirituality that began in the early 19th century, though it was exposed to the dualist Gnosis by way of the writings of orthodox Christian heresiologists, by and large rejected the disparagement of Nature and the body found in some older sources in order to embrace a way of wholeness in which the unity of all things, rather than the radical division of the dualist traditions, was central. Because the core of Gnosticism is not a historical tradition but a timeless experience of acquaintance with spiritual realities, the attitude of the Gnostic revival is significant in this context; a Gnostic of the early 19th century, or for that matter of the early 21st, has as much access to gnosis and as much right to speak for the tradition of Gnosticism as their equivalents in the second century.

No two contemporary Gnostic movements have exactly the same understanding of gnosis. This is as it should be, since the Gnostic orientation toward personal experience and direct acquaintance with spiritual realities precludes any drift toward uniformity. The way of understanding gnosis and Gnosticism presented here does not claim to apply to any part of the movement except that embodied in the Gnostic Celtic Church. Nor, for that matter, should it be seen as any sort of constraint on the personal experience of any member of that church. Rather, it provides a shared language of symbol and concept through which the teachings and the training program of the GCC can be communicated and discussed.

Some of the elements of that shared language have been discussed already in the definition of the teachings of the Gnostic Celtic Church as "Gnostic, Universalist, and Pelagian," given earlier in this book. Two additional elements deserve discussion here. They are, first, the Doctrine of One, which is a core part of the inheritance received by the GCC from its roots in the Universal Gnostic Church; and second, the teaching of the two currents, which is an important part of the traditions handed down to the GCC from the Druid Revival.

The Doctrine of One

The Universal Gnostic Church, in its embrace of a spiritual vision rooted in personal acquaintance with divine realities, discarded early on most of the formal creed it inherited from its historical roots in the Universalist Church. From the alternative spirituality of the early twentieth century, however, the UGC embraced one core teaching, commonly known then and since as the Doctrine of

One. This doctrine is simply the teaching that all things are one: that everything in existence is an expression or manifestation of one ultimate reality, the "One Thing" of the old alchemists, from which all other things come forth.

It is easy to misunderstand this doctrine, and even easier to miss its deeper implications. Many people assume, for example, that the single ultimate reality proposed by the Doctrine of One must be the same as the one god or goddess of today's popular monotheistic faiths. Those who find such faiths appropriate to their own Awen are free to make that equation, but those who follow a different vision of the divine are equally free to set it aside in favor of some other way of making sense of the relation between gods and the unity of all things. Whether the One is a personal or an impersonal presence is a matter for each individual to determine. The Gnostic Celtic Church thus leaves this, as all other theological questions, to the personal experience and understanding of the individual.

All that is stated by the Doctrine of One is that all things derive from the same transcendent source and are thus, at some deep level, akin. The importance of this doctrine is precisely that it challenges the most problematic form of dualism that runs through the religious imagination of our age: the claim that all phenomena can be divided neatly into those that participate in the spiritual dimension of existence and those that do not. Spirit and matter, sacred and secular, mind and body, god and devil, salvation and damnation: in these forms and many others, the popular dualisms of our time wall up the spiritual side of reality in an assortment of imaginary ghettos and then proceed to picture the rest of the cosmos as a lump of mere matter, desacralized, disenchanted, and stripped of all claim to inherent value.

The Gnostic Celtic Church holds no quarrel with those who embrace popular dualisms of this sort—they have as much right to their belief as we have to ours—but the vision of spirituality central to the GCC's work, and more generally to the traditions of the Universal Gnosis and those of the Druid Revival, follows a different path. The Doctrine of One teaches us to see the presence of the Divine in every phenomenon, and to recognize a kinship among all beings that admits of no exceptions. If all things are manifestations of one ultimate reality, those things that have commonly been despised by dualistic faiths are just as much revelations of that reality, and thus just as worthy of contemplation and reverence, as those things that have commonly been exalted by these same faiths.

Nor, the Doctrine of One suggests, is it enough to follow the currently popular practice of standing one or more traditional dualisms on its head, and affirming what some older tradition condemns while condemning what it affirms. A dualism with all the signs reversed is still a dualism. The Doctrine of One challenges us to see the universe whole, as a single revelation of reality, and thus to dissolve the imaginary barrier that separates the spiritual from the supposedly nonspiritual and see, as the Taoist sage Chuang Tsu saw, the eternal Tao made manifest even in shards of broken pottery and lumps of excrement.

In adopting the Doctrine of One, the Universal Gnostic Church thus placed a twofold significance in its own name. The church and the traditions descended from it affirm *a universal gnosis*—that is, a gnosis that is freely and universally available to all beings, rather than being arbitrarily restricted to a minority of elite souls. Here the roots of the Universal Gnostic Church and its daughter traditions in the old Universalist movement can be seen clearly, for it was the distinctive teaching of Universalism that every soul would eventually be saved by the infinite grace of a just and loving God. Translate this same insight into the Pelagian terms the Gnostic Celtic Church finds more useful as a language for its work, and the way to gnosis becomes an ever-present reality manifested in all things, and thus available at every moment to all beings.

It is on the basis of this insight that the church and its daughter traditions also affirm *a gnosis of the universe*—that is, a gnosis that is manifest within the universe we experience, the universe of Nature and of matter, rather than being rooted in a rejection of Nature and the material world, as some other traditions propose. Here the bridge that would eventually connect the Universal Gnostic Church to the Ancient Order of Druids in America can be traced, for it is a central insight of the Druid Revival traditions that the divine is revealed to the human mind most clearly, and with the least interference on the part of human bias and prejudice, in the phenomena of Nature. Mystics and philosophers of an earlier time once spoke of the Book of Nature, meaning by it all natural phenomena, which could be read as scripture by those versed in its wordless language; this same insight underlies the implications of this second affirmation.

Both these affirmations unfold naturally from the Doctrine of One. If all beings without exception are expressions of one ultimate reality, sharing a fundamental kinship with each other and with the transcendental ground of their own existence, then it is hard to conceive of any reason why only a certain subset of beings should be permitted to attain personal acquaintance with the divine, while others should be denied that experience. Equally, if all things without exception manifest the ultimate reality from which they all come forth, then it is hard to conceive of any reason why natural phenomena should not be recognized, contemplated, and revered as the most readily accessible revelations of the one reality that gave them birth.

It is from reflections such as these that the Gnostic Celtic Church derives one of its core themes, the Gnosis of Nature. We do not define the transcendental ground of being behind all appearances by any conceptual formula—we find it more useful to leave such formulations to the insight and personal experience of the individual—but we suggest that this ground of being may be approached, contemplated, and embraced through its reflection in Nature. By studying Nature, contemplating Nature, celebrating the cycles of Nature, and recognizing and honoring our place in Nature through practical as well as ceremonial actions, we pursue the personal acquaintance with spiritual realities that has been central to every expression of the Gnostic tradition.

The Two Currents

To speak of Nature in today's world, however, is to risk running afoul of one of the more common of the popular dualisms in contemporary life: the one which divides the universe into natural and supernatural realms. It is a fine irony that this division is accepted with equal enthusiasm by followers of fundamentalist religions and believers in modern scientific-materialist atheism, who agree on so little else. To be sure, religious fundamentalists glorify the supernatural and condemn the natural as lower and probably sinful, while scientific atheists glorify the natural and condemn the supernatural as nonexistent, but the reality of the division itself remains very nearly unquestioned.

In contemporary Druidry, as in most of the world's spiritual traditions outside the modern Western world, the concept of the supernatural as separate from the natural makes no sense at all. What fundamentalists and atheists call "natural," from this older and arguably wiser standpoint, is simply one arbitrary subset of the whole fabric of the cosmos, while what both call "supernatural" is another subset, overlapping so thoroughly with the first that no firm line can or should be drawn between them. This implies that patterns of natural order may be used to make sense of seemingly supernatural realities, but it also implies that what we call the natural world is pervaded by what current thought considers to be supernatural forces.

The most important of these forces is one that has a name in nearly all the world's languages and a place in nearly all the world's spiritual traditions—the exceptions in both cases being those of the modern industrial West. This is the life force, a subtle energy-like presence (it is not energy in the strictly scientific sense of the word) that pervades all things and gives them consciousness, life and power. Hindu philosophy calls the life force prana, Chinese physicians and martial artists call it qi, the Hebrew text of the Old Testament calls it ruach, and so on. In the Welsh folk traditions from which the Druid Revival drew much of its lore, the term for the life force is nwyfre (pronounced NOO-iv-ruh).

Nwyfre is everywhere and in all things, and according to Druid Revival teachings it is the means by which most of the apparently miraculous phenomena of religion, mysticism, and magic are accomplished. It is not merely a symbol, for it can be experienced directly by those who learn how to do so, as (for example) students of yoga, Asian martial arts, and many other activities involving the life force learn to do. Each spiritual tradition has its own distinct ways of accessing, directing and using nwyfre, and its own preferred sources or nwyfre on which their practitioners draw. In the work of the GCC and the AODA alike, the two sources of nwyfre that are principally used are the solar and telluric currents.

According to the traditional teaching, the solar current has its source in the sun and descends from above. It flows wherever light from the sky can reach, and even penetrates a short distance down into the soil. The other planets of the solar system reflect the solar current to earth just as they reflect the sun's light, and their cycles shape the flow of the solar current in ways that can be tracked by a variety of traditional systems for understanding the cycles of time. The solar current's more common symbols in myth and legend are birds such as the eagle, the hawk, and the heron. Occult writings sometimes call it *aud* or *od*, and in alchemy it is the Sun. Its primary symbol in Druid lore is the circle, representing the sun's orb; it is symbolically masculine, and its color is gold.

The telluric current takes its name from Tellus, an old name for the earth; it rises from below. It takes its form and character from the landscape the way the solar current takes its character from the turning planets, and is thus defined by space rather than time; where the student of the solar current watches the turning heavens, the student of the telluric current learns to read the patterns of the landscape. The serpent and the dragon are the most common symbols of the telluric current in myth and legend. Its names in occult lore include the secret fire, the dragon current, and *aub* or *ob*, and in alchemy it is Mercury. Its primary symbol in Druid lore is the triangle, representing its fiery and transforming nature; it is symbolically feminine, and its color is green.

A great many religious and philosophical traditions draw on one of these two currents while rejecting the other. The contemporary religious mainstream calls on the solar current when it makes use of any subtle forces at all; thus it envisions God "up above" as the ultimate reality creating and manipulating a passive material world "down below," and portrays the fiery, serpentine telluric current as the Devil in Hell. The scientific-materialist atheism that gives today's mainstream religion its equal and opposite social force, in turn, envisions the ultimate reality as matter and energy "down below" struggling up toward life and intelligence in a universe in which "up above" refers only to empty space.

Spiritual traditions that assign equal value both sides of this equation are a distinct minority, but they do exist. Taoism, with its cosmology of balance between yin and yang, is among the best known. Shinto, the traditional polytheist faith of Japan, is another, and the ancient traditions of alchemy provide yet another example— "as above, so below," the alchemist's watchword, is among the best known expressions of the path of balance that is shared by these traditions. Druidry is another such tradition. Again, the Gnostic Celtic Church has no quarrel with those who reject this way of balance and prefer to see the universe in terms of a struggle between good and evil, truth and ignorance, or some other dualism; we simply choose a different path.

While the two currents have their symbolic importance, it is also important to recognize that, like nwyfre, they are not simply symbols. They are realities that can be experienced directly by human consciousness. They are also sources of subtle energy that can empower ritual and other forms of inner work. Many people have experienced the rush of vitality that comes from opening the body and mind to the presence and power of the Sun, and the very different but equally strong sense of wholeness and balance that comes from close contact with the Earth. These experiences are valid and powerful in their own right, but they are also clues to other possibilities that open up when Sun and Earth, Above and Below, are brought into living balance through the tools of meditation and ritual.

In the work of the Gnostic Celtic Church, the most important of the possibilities that unfolds from an understanding of the two currents is the potential for creating a third current, which is called the lunar current. The lunar current is called aur and or in occult writings. Its primary symbol in magical lore is the crescent moon, and its mythic symbols include the egg, the jewel, the sacred cup, and the child. It mediates between solar and telluric currents in the same way that the moon mediates between sun and earth, and its symbolic color is white.

Unlike the solar and telluric currents, the lunar current is not always present; it may emerge spontaneously by contact between the other two currents in just the right conditions, but in most cases it has to be made, by deliberate action, out of the balanced fusion of the solar and telluric forces. To bring it into being, according to a traditional teaching, is the central art of an ancient system of natural magic embodied in the standing stones and earthworks of northwestern Europe and northeastern North America, and the goal of that art—a threefold blessing of fertility, healing, and the awakening of wisdom, embodied in the subtle influence of the lunar current and radiated outwards in all directions—is recalled in lightly veiled form in the legends of the Holy Grail.

The creation of the lunar current, and its wise direction as an instrument of blessing, is a central part of the work taught to priests and priestesses of the Gnostic Celtic Church. That work takes many forms, but its core expression in our teachings and practice may be found in our distinctive Communion ceremony, the heart of the GCC's ceremonial work.

Introduction to GCC Ceremonial

One of the factors that sets apart the Gnostic Celtic Church from many other alternative religious movements in contemporary society, as already mentioned, is its adoption of a regular rather than a secular model for its ordained clergy. In the conventional, secular model of ministry, which evolved in mainstream Protestant churches in the United States and has become institutionalized in American society, the distinctive work performed by the clergy focuses on performing rites of passage—"Hatch 'em, match 'em, and dispatch 'em," to borrow a joke heard tolerably often among mainstream Christian clergy—as well as weekly services for a congregation, and an assortment of sidelines ranging from counseling to various kinds of political and social activism.

No rule forbids priests and priestesses of the GCC from performing infant blessings, weddings, funeral services, or other rites of passage if work of this kind proves to be an appropriate expression of their own personal Awen. Nor are they banned from engaging in other activities common to clergy in the mainstream culture. On the other hand, no rule requires them to engage in any of these activities, and no particular stress is placed on such activities in the training for ordination that aspirants to the GCC priesthood and priesshood are required to complete. Instead of serving a congregation or a community of human beings, priests and priestesses in the GCC are ordained to serve the divine, and the primary form taken by this service is ceremonial and mystical in nature.

The conventional wisdom of today's society tends to assume that ceremonies are by definition empty forms, and that mysticism involves an abandonment of the outside world and its cares and concerns. The experience of billions of people over thousands of years suggests otherwise. The links between mind and mind, and between mind and matter, seem to be significantly more complex and subtle than current scientific theory allows; the collective mood swings central to mob psychology are difficult to interpret without at least considering the possibility of a collective consciousness that however briefly unites a crowd into a single meta-organism, and the

25

"vibe" or intuitively sensed quality of a place where traumatic events have taken place is something many people have experienced.

A similar effect, though more controlled and more positive, radiates outward from certain classes of ceremonial working and certain forms of mystical practice. In the teachings of the modern Druid tradition, nwyfre—the subtle life force that pervades all things—is said to mediate this process, spreading the influence of focused intention from mind to mind for good or ill. In the ceremonial work of the GCC, this effect is used deliberately; the solar and telluric currents, the two primary currents of nwyfre worked in the AODA and GCC traditions, are invoked and fused into the lunar current, and this latter flows outward to the living Earth and all that lives upon her, blessing the land to fruitfulness and offering assistance to all beings who desire to rise toward that higher mode of consciousness the Druid Revival traditions call Gwynfydd, "the radiant life."

This work of blessing is the core practice of the GCC priesthood and priesshood. Like the monastic clergy of many other spiritual traditions, the priests and priestesses of our church pursue their own ceremonial and mystical work in private, deepening their own relationships with the Divine in full awareness that the influences of their work extend outward to bring benedictions to the wider human community and the Earth. To accomplish this, the priests and priestesses of the GCC are charged with practicing a particular ceremonial working, the Communion ceremony, which is meant both to foster their own spiritual development and to offer blessings to the land and the beings, human and otherwise, who dwell upon it. The practice of the communion ceremony is not restricted to priests and priestesses; it may be performed by any person who desires to do so, and deacons in training for priesthood or priesshood are expected to perform it regularly. What distinguishes the priests and priestesses of the GCC from others is not the power to perform this ceremony but the responsibility to do so, for the benefit of the living Earth and all that lives upon her.

The Communion ceremony derives from the broader pattern of AODA ritual. Like other solitary AODA ceremonies, it begins and ends with the solitary Grove ritual, and includes the Sphere of Protection, the first ritual taught to each AODA member and the cornerstone of AODA ritual practice. The study program that leads to initiation in the First Degree of AODA, which is required for reception as a deacon in the GCC, includes daily practice of the Sphere of Protection; the study program that leads to initiation in the Second Degree of AODA, which is required for ordination as a priest or priestess, includes close study and regular practice of the solitary Grove ritual, so that any prospective priest or priestess should be well trained in the performance of these rituals. Both rituals are nonetheless printed in full later on in this book, so that priests and priestesses in training will have a convenient reference for their ceremonial work.

Alongside the elements of the Communion ceremony, three additional spiritual practices are presented to deacons in the course of their training for the GCC priesthood or priestesshood. These practices are the creation and tending of a home altar, and the practices of morning prayer and evening lection. These practices are set out in a later section of this book. While deacons who intend to seek ordination as priests or priestesses should expect to perform these practices regularly during their training, ordained priests and priestesses, bishops, and those deacons who do not intend to seek ordination may make use of them, modify them, or set them aside as their personal spiritual paths may indicate.

The following sections present the core ceremonial practices of the GCC in the order that they are learned: first, the Sphere of Protection; then the solitary Grove opening and closing ceremony; then the Communion ceremony, which takes place in an open Grove that has been purified and prepared by the Sphere of Protection; then a set of four seasonal rituals, each of which includes the three ceremonies already named.

The Gnostic Celtic Church

The Sphere of Protection

The Sphere of Protection was created in the 1970s by Dr. John Gilbert, then one of the archdruids of AODA, using material drawn from several older rituals then current in AODA practice. It has three phases: an opening, a closing, and a middle section in which the core work is done. The opening is called the Elemental Cross, the middle section is the Calling of the Elements, and the closing is the Sphere of Light.

The Sphere, as it is often called for short, was adopted almost immediately as a standard ritual by AODA and many of the esoteric traditions affiliated with it, and today is the first ritual learned and practiced by any newly initiated member of AODA. Like the comparable rituals taught and practiced in the beginning stages of other esoteric spiritual traditions—for example, the Lesser Ritual of the Pentagram in the Hermetic Order of the Golden Dawn—its obvious purpose is to purify and strengthen the subtle body of the practitioner, which it does effectively; it also has a subtler and less apparent purpose, which is to orient the practitioner in the symbolic cosmos within which the work of the tradition takes place.

The process of learning the Sphere of Protection involves a certain degree of complexity, because each person who learns and practices it is expected to enrich it with personally relevant symbolism. The details of the learning process are covered in *The Druid Magic Handbook* and will not be repeated here. The version given here is an example rather than a specific form to be followed letter by letter, and the particular set of divine names and symbols may be used but are not mandatory; readers familiar with other forms of the same ritual will find that the one given here differs from these others in several respects.

The wording that invokes the blessing of the elements for the Grove, however, should be used either as given or with minor modifications in GCC workings, especially in the Communion ceremony, and the phrasing of the invocations of the telluric, solar, and lunar currents should not be changed unless the student has very good reason to do so. The three currents are the main sources of power in GCC ritual, and the Sphere of Protection ritual is the way these powers are welcomed into the Grove and linked to its symbolism and ceremonial formulae.

The Elemental Cross

(To begin this version of the Sphere, stand at the north side of the altar, facing south, in performing the Communion Ceremony or any other GCC ritual, and in the center of the room, facing south, in a solitary practice of the Sphere of Protection alone. Imagine the Sun standing at zenith high above your head, and an equivalent sphere of silver-green fire, which the heart of the Earth, far below your feet. Be aware of yourself standing between these two spheres.

(Now bring your arms up from your sides in an arc, bringing them together above your head. Imagine a ray of light descending from the Sun to your hands. Draw the hands down to your forehead, joining palm to palm, and imagine the light descending with the movement to form a sphere of light, like a star, within your head. As your hands pause before your forehead, say:)

Hu the Mighty, Great Druid God.

(Draw the hands down to the region of your solar plexus, keeping the palms joined. Imagine the light descending to your solar plexus, and forming a second sphere of light there, then descending through you and beyond you to the sphere of fire at the heart of the Earth. As your hands pause at your solar plexus, say:)

Hesus of the Oaks, Chief of Tree-Spirits.

(Leaving your left hand where it is, at your solar plexus, pivot your right arm outwards at the elbow, so that your right arm ends up angling down and outwards in a straight line from your shoulder. Imagine a ray of light shooting out from the sphere of light at your solar plexus, straight outward into infinite distance to your right. Say:)

Ceridwen the Wise, Keeper of the Cauldron.

(Repeat the same gesture with your left hand, so that both arms now slope down and outward from your shoulders, forming with your body the image of the Three Rays. Imagine a ray of light shooting out from the sphere of light at your solar plexus, straight outward into infinite distance to your left. Say:)

Niwalen of the Flowers, Child of Spring.

(Cross your arms across your chest, right over left, and imagine twin rays of light shooting out from the sphere of light at your solar plexus in front of you and behind you into infinite distance. Say:)

May the powers of Nature bless and protect this Grove, this day and always.

(This completes the Elemental Cross.)

The Calling of the Elements

(Go to the eastern quarter of the Grove, and trace the symbol of the element of air, which is a circle with a line extending straight upwards from its uppermost point. Trace the circle first, clockwise from the uppermost point, then trace the line; this is the summoning mode of drawing the symbol. Imagine the symbol being traced in a line of golden light, and the circle filling in with golden light.

(As you do so, imagine a scene beyond the symbol corresponding to the symbolism of the east—for example, a spring meadow at daybreak with the Sun rising, a fresh wind blowing toward you with the scent of grass and flowers, great billowing clouds in the distance with their edges turned golden by the Sun's rays, and so on. Say:)

By the yellow gate of the rushing winds and the hawk of May in the heights of morning, I invoke the air, its gods, its spirits, and its powers. May the powers of Air bless and protect this Grove, and further its work.

(If the ritual is being performed as part of the Communion ceremony, go on to say:)

May all the powers of the Eastern quarter be welcome to this ceremony of Communion.

(Now trace the same symbol again, but trace the circle counterclockwise from the uppermost point, then draw the line upwards as before; this is the banishing mode of drawing the symbol. Say:)

I thank the air for its gifts. And with the help of the powers of air, I banish from within and around this Grove all harmful and disturbing influences and every imbalance of the nature of air. I banish these things far from this place.

(Go to the southern quarter of the Grove, and trace the symbol of the element of fire, which is an equilateral triangle, point up. Trace this clockwise from the uppermost point to summon; imagine the symbol being drawn in red light, then filled in with red light.

33

(As you do so, imagine a scene beyond the symbol corresponding to the symbolism of the south—for example, a desert like those in the American southwest at noon on a summer's day, with red rock mesas in the middle distance and reddish sand close by, the sun blazing down overhead, the heat making the air shimmer and radiating toward you, and so on. Say:)

By the red gate of the bright flames and the white stag of the summer greenwood, I invoke the fire, its gods, its spirits, and its powers. May the powers of fire bless and protect this Grove, and further its work.

(If the ritual is being performed as part of the Communion ceremony, go on to say:)

May all the powers of the Southern quarter be welcome to this ceremony of Communion.

(Now trace the same symbol again, counterclockwise from the uppermost point, to banish. Say:)

I thank the fire for its gifts. And with the help of the powers of fire, I banish from within and around this Grove all harmful and disturbing influences and every imbalance of the nature of fire. I banish these things far from this place.

(Go to the western quarter of the Grove, and trace the symbol of the element of water, which is an equilateral triangle, point down. Trace this clockwise from the lowermost point to summon; imagine the symbol being drawn in blue light, then filled in with blue light.

(As you do so, imagine a scene beyond the symbol corresponding to the symbolism of the west—for example, an ocean beach at sunset on an autumn day, with great waves rolling toward you from out of the distance, rain falling from clouds overhead, the setting sun just visible on the horizon through a gap in the clouds and its rays making the clouds and sea glow, and so on. Say:)

By the blue gate of the mighty waters and the salmon of wisdom in the sacred pool, I invoke the water, its gods, its spirits, and its powers. May the powers of water bless and protect this Grove, and further its work.

(If the ritual is being performed as part of the Communion ceremony, go on to say:)

May all the powers of the Western quarter be welcome to this ceremony of Communion.

(Now trace the same symbol again, counterclockwise from the lowermost point, to banish. Say:)

I thank the water for its gifts. And with the help of the powers of water, I banish from within and around this Grove all harmful and disturbing influences and every imbalance of the nature of water. I banish these things far from this place.

(Go to the northern quarter of the Grove, and trace the symbol of the element of earth, which is a circle with a line extending down from its lowermost point — the mirror image of the symbol of air. Trace this clockwise from the lowermost point, and then draw the line downward, to summon; imagine the symbol being drawn in green light, then filled in with green light.

(As you do so, imagine a scene beyond the symbol corresponding to the symbolism of the north — for example, a forest scene at midnight in winter, with snow on the ground and the trees, the moon and stars shining brilliantly in a clear night sky, distant mountains beyond them with their peaks illuminated by the moonlight, and so on. Say:)

By the green gate of the tall stones and the great bear of the starry heavens, I invoke the earth, its gods, its spirits, and its powers. May the powers of earth bless and protect this Grove, and further its work.

(If the ritual is being performed as part of the Communion ceremony, go on to say:)

May all the powers of the Northern quarter be welcome to this ceremony of Communion.

(Now trace the same symbol again, drawing the circle counterclockwise from the lowermost point and then the line down from it, to banish. Say:)

I thank the earth for its gifts. And with the help of the powers of earth, I banish from within and around this Grove all harmful and disturbing influences and every imbalance of the nature of earth. I banish these things far from this place.

(Go to the north of the altar and face south. Trace a clockwise circle around the upper surface of the altar; imagine it traced in orange light, the rich orange of autumn leaves, and then fill it with the same color. Then imagine the circle descending through the altar until it is several yards down into the earth beneath you.

(As you do this, imagine the soil and stone beneath you, reaching down all the way to the green fire at the Earth's heart. Feel its stability, its richness, its immense and unhuman power, and so on. Say:)

By the orange gate of the land beneath this Grove and the power of the telluric current, I invoke Spirit Below, its gods, its spirits, and its powers. May a ray of the telluric current bless and protect this Grove, and further its work.

(Imagine a ray of silver-green flame rising up from the earth's center to the altar, coming to a halt just below the altar's surface. Say:)

I thank Spirit Below for its gifts.

(Trace a clockwise circle in the air high above the altar, imagining it traced in purple light, and then fill it with the same color. Then imagine the circle rising up in the air until it is several yards above the altar.

(As you do this, imagine the heavens above you, luminous with stars and galaxies, extending up beyond the reach of your mind's eye. The Sun shines in the midst of all, directly above your head. Feel the beauty, silence, and vastness of the cosmos, and so on. Say:)

By the purple gate of the skies above this Grove and the power of the solar current, I invoke Spirit Above, its gods, its spirits, and its powers. May a ray of the solar current bless and protect this Grove, and further its work.

> *(Imagine a ray of golden light from the Sun high above you, descending to the altar, and coming to a halt just above the altar's surface. Say:)*

I thank Spirit Above for its gifts.

> *(Now be aware of the six symbols of the elements in the six directions of space surrounding the Grove. Say:)*

By the six powers here invoked and here present, and by the grand word by which the worlds were made—AWEN

> *(chanting this word Ah-Oh-En, stretching out the vowels)—*

I invoke Spirit Within. May a ray of the lunar current bless and protect this Grove, and further its work.

> *(If there is an altar, touch it with your right hand.)*

May it establish a sphere of protection around this Grove and all within it.

> *(This completes the Calling of the Elements.)*

The Sphere of Light

(This phase of the ritual uses words and gestures only at its conclusion. The rest of the work is done solely by the imagination.

(Imagine the solar and telluric currents coming into contact at the top of the altar and forming a sphere of brilliant white light that surrounds the altar top and includes the four cauldrons. See the colored light from each cauldron radiating into the larger sphere of white light, so that it shimmers with rainbow colors.

(Next, imagine the sphere of light expanding outward until it surrounds the Grove and all within it. Take your time at this visualization, and build up the image as strongly and solidly as you are able. Concentrate on the idea that the sphere forms a barrier impenetrable to any hostile or harmful influence, a protective wall within which the work of the Grove may go on unhindered.

(When you have established the sphere as firmly as you can, cross your arms across your chest and say:)

I thank the powers for their blessings.

(Then proceed to the ceremony, or if the Sphere of Protection is being practiced by itself, pause for a few minutes, feeling the energies you have invoked, and then release the imagery from your mind, write up the experience in your practice journal, and go on with your day.)

Solitary Grove Ceremony

The solitary Grove ceremony is an adaptation and simplification of the standard AODA Grove opening and closing, and it provides the ceremonial framework within which all of the GCC ceremonial work is performed. Though it is normally learned after the Sphere of Protection, the opening half of the Grove ceremony comes first in the practice of ceremony, with the Sphere included as its final act.

The Grove is always imagined as a clearing in the forest into which pathways enter through three gates, one in the east, one in the south, and one in the west. From the east come members of the Candidate Grade of AODA and guests who are not members of the order. From the south come members of the First Degree of AODA, and from the west come members of the Second and Third Degrees. More information on the symbolism and imagery of the Grove in AODA tradition may be found in *The Druid Grove Handbook*.

The Grove ceremony should be done in a room or other place where there is ample space to move around an altar set up in the center. The altar itself may be anything from a purpose-built wooden structure to a folding TV tray draped with a white cloth. It should have four cauldrons on it—one with incense in the east, one with a candle or lamp in the south, one with water in the west, and one with salt in the north. (*The cauldrons with incense and flame should have a layer of clean sand in the bottom to insulate the altar surface from the heat.*) In an AODA ritual, a sickle and a sprig of mistletoe are normally placed at the center of the altar; in most GCC rituals, by contrast, the chalice and paten of the Communion ceremony normally fill the same central place.

SOLITARY GROVE OPENING

(Before beginning a ceremony, put the altar cloth and any decorations on the altar, and arrange the four cauldrons. Light the incense and the lamp, and then go to the edge of the area where you'll be performing the ceremony. Take a few moments to clear your mind of unrelated thoughts and feelings.

(Then, when you are ready to begin, enter the circle through whichever gate your degree entitles you to use, then go around to the north side of the altar, where you face south. Raise your right hand palm forward to salute the Spiritual Sun, which is always symbolically at high noon in the southern sky, and say:)

Let the powers be present as I am about to open a Grove of Druids in this place. *(Pause.)*

The first duty of Druids assembled in the Sacred Grove is to proclaim peace to the four quarters of the world, for without peace our work cannot proceed.
(Circle around to the east. Raise your right hand palm outward to salute the direction, and say:)

I proclaim peace in the east.
(Proceed to the south and do the same thing, saying:)

I proclaim peace in the south.
(Proceed to the west, and do the same thing, saying:)

I proclaim peace in the west.
(Proceed to the north and do the same thing, saying:)

I proclaim peace in the north.
(Advance to the north side of the altar, facing south across it. Say:)

The four quarters are at peace and the work of the Grove may proceed. Let this Grove and all within it be purified with air.
(Go to the eastern side of the altar, pick up the cauldron with the incense, and carry it to the eastern edge of the space. Pause there, holding the cauldron out as though offering the incense, and then walk in a clockwise circle once around the outer edge of the space, tracing a circle around the Grove with the cauldron. When you've come back around to the east, return the cauldron to the altar.

(While you do this, visualize the following. When you hold the cauldron as though offering the incense, imagine a current of yellow light streaming in from the east and forming a sphere of yellow light around the cauldron. As you carry the cauldron around the Grove, imagine the cauldron tracing a line of yellow light in a circle around the outside of the Grove. When you carry the cauldron back to the altar, see it trace a line of yellow light in from the edge to the altar, and see the sphere of yellow light remaining with the cauldron on the altar.

(When you have finished, say:)

Let this Grove and all within it be purified with fire.

(Go to the southern side of the altar, pick up the cauldron with the flame, and carry it to the southern edge of the space. Pause there, holding the cauldron out as though offering the flame, and then walk in a clockwise circle once around the outer edge of the space, tracing a circle around the Grove with the cauldron. When you've come back around to the south, return the cauldron to the altar.

(While you do this, visualize the following. When you hold the cauldron as though offering the incense, imagine a current of red light streaming in from the south and forming a sphere of red light around the cauldron. As you carry the cauldron around the Grove, imagine the cauldron tracing a line of red light in a circle around the outside of the Grove. When you carry the cauldron back to the altar, see it trace a line of red light in from the edge to the altar, and see the sphere of red light remaining with the cauldron on the altar.

(When you have finished, say:)

Let this Grove and all within it be purified with water.

(Go to the western side of the altar, pick up the cauldron with the water, and carry it to the western edge of the space. Pause there, holding the cauldron out as though offering the water, and then walk in a clockwise circle once around the outer edge of the space, tracing a circle around the Grove with the cauldron. When you've come back around to the west, return the cauldron to the altar.

(While you do this, visualize the following. When you hold the cauldron as though offering the water, imagine a current of blue light streaming in from the west and forming a sphere of blue light around the cauldron. As you carry the cauldron around the Grove, imagine the cauldron tracing a line of blue light in a circle around the outside of the Grove. When you carry the cauldron back to the altar, see it trace a line of blue light in from the edge to the altar, and see the sphere of blue light remaining with the cauldron on the altar.

(When you have finished, say:)

Let this Grove and all within it be purified with earth.

(Go to the northern side of the altar, pick up the cauldron with the salt, and carry it to the northern edge of the space. Pause there, holding the cauldron out as though offering the salt, and then walk in a clockwise circle once around the outer edge of the space, tracing a circle around the Grove with the cauldron. When you've come back around to the north, return the cauldron to the altar.

(While you do this, visualize the following. When you hold the cauldron as though offering the salt, imagine a current of green light streaming in from the north and forming a sphere of green light around the cauldron. As you carry the cauldron around the Grove, imagine the cauldron tracing a line of green light in a circle around the outside of the Grove. When you carry the cauldron back to the altar, see it trace a line of green light in from the edge to the altar, and see the sphere of green light remaining with the cauldron on the altar.

(When you have finished, say:)

I invoke the blessing of the holy powers with the words that have been the bond among all Druids:

Grant, O holy ones, thy protection;
And in protection, strength;
And in strength, understanding;
And in understanding, knowledge;
And in knowledge, the knowledge of justice;
And in the knowledge of justice, the love of it;
And in that love, the love of all existences;

And in the love of all existences, the love of Earth our mother and all goodness.

(When you've finished the prayer, chant the word Awen three times:)

AWEN, AWEN, AWEN

(Draw the word out into its three syllables – Ah-Oh-En – and let it resonate throughout your body and the Grove. Then perform the complete Sphere of Protection ceremony, as given earlier in this book. This completes the opening ceremony.)

SOLITARY GROVE CLOSING

(When you have finished whatever ceremony you are performing, rise and go to the north side of the altar, facing south across it. Say:)

Let the powers be attentive as I am about to close a Grove of Druids in this place.

(Go to the eastern side of the altar. Take the cauldron with the incense to the east, and hold it outward as though offering the incense, as in the opening. Say:)

With thanks I release the powers of air to their rightful places. May there be peace in the east.

(As you say this, imagine the yellow light that surrounds the cauldron flowing back to its sources in the east. When this is finished, return the cauldron to its place on the altar, and go to the southern side of the altar. Take the cauldron with the flame to the south, and hold it outward as though offering the flame, as in the opening. Say:)

With thanks I release the powers of fire to their rightful places. May there be peace in the south.

(As you say this, imagine the red light that surrounds the cauldron flowing back to its sources in the south. When this is finished, return the cauldron to its place on the altar, and go to the western side of the altar. Take the cauldron with the water to the west, and hold it outward as though offering the water, as in the opening. Say:)

With thanks I release the powers of water to their rightful places. May there be peace in the west.

> *(As you say this, imagine the blue light that surrounds the cauldron flowing back to its sources in the west. When this is finished, return the cauldron to its place on the altar, and go to the northern side of the altar. Take the cauldron with the salt to the north, and hold it outward as though offering the salt, as in the opening. Say:)*

With thanks I release the powers of earth to their rightful places. May there be peace in the north.

> *(As you say this, imagine the green light that surrounds the cauldron flowing back to its sources in the north. When this is finished, return the cauldron to its place on the altar, and remain at the northern side of the altar, facing south. Say:)*

Peace prevails in the four quarters and throughout the Grove. Let any power remaining from this working be returned to the Earth for her blessing.

> *(Any ritual working leaves some energy behind it, and this can usually be sensed as a mood, a feeling, or a subtle sense of presence in the space. Imagine this flowing inward toward the altar, down through it to the earth, and then down to the earth's center. Keep concentrating on this until the ritual space feels clear of any leftover energy. Then say:)*

I now invoke the Sword of Swords.

> *(Visualize a great medieval sword hovering in the air before you, point down, and raise your hand in salute. Say the following incantation:)*

**From the rising Sun, three rays of light;
From the living Earth, three stones of witness;
From the eye and the mind and the hand of wisdom, three rowan staves of all knowledge.
From the fire of the Sun, the forge;
From the bones of the Earth, the steel;**

From the hand of the wise, the making;
From these, Excalibur.
By the Sword of Swords, I pledge my faithful service to the
living Earth, our home and mother.

(Chant the word Awen once, drawing out the syllables Ah-Oh-En:)
AWEN.

*(As you chant the word, imagine the sword dissolving into pure
light, which draws together into the image of the Spiritual Sun,
standing high in the south. Lower your hand, and leave the altar;
walk in a clockwise circle around the Grove to whichever gate your
degree entitles you to use, and exit the Grove. This concludes the
closing ceremony.)*

The Gnostic Celtic Church

Communion Ceremony

The Communion ceremony, as already noted, forms the core religious practice of the GCC, the focus of its ceremonial work and the primary means by which its priests and priestesses make manifest the influences of the living spirit in the world of matter. Like equivalent ceremonies in other spiritual traditions, it centers on a ritual process by which food and drink become the vessels for spiritual potencies, and are then reverently consumed by the participants in the ceremony.

It is often assumed that ceremonies of this kind are unique to Christianity and have their original form in the Orthodox or Catholic Mass. The Christian communion service, though, was powerfully influenced by older traditions of communion services and sacrificial meals, and equivalent ceremonies were found in a wide range of spiritual traditions in the ancient world. The worshippers of the god Mithras, to name only one example, are known to have celebrated a communion service in which bread and wine were consecrated and consumed.

Behind such ceremonies lie archaic traditions of sacrifice, in which animals were offered up to deities and their flesh roasted and consumed by the worshippers, as part of a wider custom of food offerings rooted in the universal custom of sharing food as a sign of hospitality and respect. It is an irony of history that so many Christians who talk of "being washed in the blood of the Lamb" have forgotten that this metaphor was a living reality in the time of Jesus, when worshippers—almost certainly including Jesus himself—offered actual lambs in sacrifice at the temple in Jerusalem, and were daubed with their blood as a sign of purification.

Even in ancient times, however, animal sacrifice was only one of many options, and shifts in custom and consciousness made other ceremonial forms more appropriate to most people. The Christian communion service and its equivalents in other traditions were in large part a response to that shift. More recently, communion rituals such as the Communion of the Elements practiced by the Hermetic Order of the Golden Dawn, the Order of Worship of the Reformed

Druids of North America, and the Sangreal Sacrament practiced by students of William Gray's Sangreal tradition, have had a significant role in contemporary alternative spirituality, as has the quasi-communion of cakes and ale that plays a role in many Wiccan rites. It is as part of the modern rediscovery of this ancient mode of worship and work that the GCC's Communion ceremony has its place.

The teachings of the Gnosis of Nature presented earlier in this book provide the core on which the GCC Communion ceremony is founded. The two primary currents of nwyfre or life force in the world of human experience—the solar current descending from the heart of the Sun, and the telluric current ascending from the heart of the Earth—are the two sources of spiritual power invoked in the Communion ceremony, and their union into the lunar current is the goal of the work. Depending on the preferences of the priest or priestess performing the rite, gods or goddesses may be invoked, or the pure impersonal currents may be called into play; this freedom allows the widest possible range for the personal and experiential side of the work, while still working within a common ritual framework.

REQUIREMENTS OF THE CEREMONY

The GCC Communion ceremony, unlike some other communion rituals, is not primarily an act of public worship. Though the priest or priestess who celebrates the ceremony is free to invite others to witness the work and partake of the communion, he or she is also wholly free to celebrate it in solitude, and under most circumstances this will be found the most practical option. Those whose attendance is necessary for the ceremony are not human beings but the holy powers of Nature, and in particular the solar and telluric currents, the powers of the elements, and whatever deities and spirits the priest or priestess may choose to invoke.

The material requirements of the ceremony are relatively simple. Like the ordinary AODA solitary Grove ceremony, it should be performed in a room or other space with an altar at the center, ample room to move around the altar, and a chair in the north where the celebrant will sit for reading and meditation. An altar cloth, white or colored according to the seasons (as described later), should be placed on the altar, and on this the four cauldrons used in the Grove ritual should be in their usual places.

The garb of the celebrant may be determined according to individual Awen, though a plain white robe with a cord belt, the standard dress in AODA ritual, is wholly suitable for the Communion ceremony as well. If the celebrant has been ordained as a priest or priestess in the GCC, the green stole conferred at ordination should certainly be worn.

In place of the sickle and mistletoe normally used in the Grove ceremony, however, a chalice and a paten (a small plate for the bread) occupy the center of the altar. These should be of pottery or stoneware if possible, to represent the Earth, and should be of a simple design. Chalices and patens of the kind used in Catholic practice are emphatically not suited to this ceremony,* any more than are the elaborate arrangements made to keep the bread and wine of the Catholic service separate from the rest of the material world; in a tradition that affirms the holiness of Nature and the presence of spiritual powers throughout the material world, such habits would be utterly out of place.

In addition to these, two cruets or small vessels, for wine and water respectively, are used. These should also be of pottery or earthenware if possible. Finally, when the ceremony is performed indoors and the wine remaining at the end of the ceremony may not be poured directly on the Earth in offering, a bowl or cauldron is placed at the foot of the altar; it may be of any convenient material.

The material substances that are to be consecrated and consumed in the ceremony are bread and wine—bread as a vessel for the telluric current, and wine as a vessel for the solar current; the wine is mixed with water, to represent the alchemical fusion of the red and white dragon currents, symbolized also by the Red and White Wells of Glastonbury that play a significant role in the legends of the Holy Grail. It is best for the bread to be made from some kind of grain, and the wine fermented from some kind of fruit; wheat and grape are by no means required, though they may certainly be used if desired. Should the priest or priestess, or any other person partaking of the communion, have dietary issues that would preclude using grain or fermented fruit wine, it is wholly acceptable to find a substitute; the symbol is more important than the substance, and the powers that brought the worlds into being are after all more than capable of bringing themselves into full manifestation in any material substance whatsoever.

It is customary in the GCC to receive communion by intinction—that is, by having each person who partakes of communion take a portion of bread in his or her hand, dip the bread into the wine in the chalice, and then place the wine-soaked bread in his or her own mouth. This is considerably more sanitary than sharing a common cup, and considerably less cumbersome than using a separate cup for each participant. Furthermore, it has an important symbolic meaning.

Anyone who partakes of the communion by intinction is an active participant, not merely a passive recipient in the ceremony. He or she personally performs the crucial action of the ritual, the union of the material vessels of the solar and telluric currents. It is a reminder of the Pelagian side of the GCC's teachings: no one attains the state of conscious union with the source of being—the state that Christian teachings call salvation, Eastern teachings term enlightenment, and Druid lore calls Gwynfydd—by another's actions or another's merit. All of us must accomplish that for ourselves, and all of us are capable of accomplishing that for ourselves.

In addition to the items just named, a book should be chosen to provide a brief reading for meditation. The lection, as the reading is called, is to be freely chosen by the celebrant according to his or her personal Awen. It should be relatively short, no more than a paragraph or two at most, and generally less than that; its purpose is to provide seed thoughts for meditation. Among the sources that provide suitable readings for the lection are books of spiritual philosophy, such as the Tao Te Ching or The Book of Druidry; books of ecological wisdom, such as Walden or A Sand County Almanac; books of poetry, particularly those inspired by nature; and books of nature study, especially those suited to the local environment and rich in vivid descriptions.

Before the opening of the ceremony, the lection text is set next to the celebrant's chair. The chalice is placed on the center of the altar and the paten placed atop the chalice. The bread is set on the paten, and the cruets of wine and water are placed on the western side of the altar, between the cauldron of water and the altar's northern edge. The candle in the fire cauldron and the incense in the air cauldron are lit, and the ceremony begins with the solitary Grove opening ceremony and the Sphere of Protection ritual, which have already been given.

COMMUNION CEREMONY

(After you have finished the solitary Grove opening ceremony and the Sphere of Protection ritual, you are standing at the north side of the altar, facing south. Go to the seat in the north and be seated. Open the Lection text, and say:)

The lection for this ceremony is from *(name of book or other source).*
(At this point read the text aloud. If the celebrant is alone, the text may be read in a quiet voice; if there are others present, it should be read clearly, so that all may hear it. It should be read slowly, to allow the celebrant and any others present to pay close attention to each word and phrase, and gather one or more seed thoughts for meditation. When it is done, pause and then say:)

May the holy powers enlighten my mind (or: our minds).
(Set the text aside, and enter into meditation, using by preference the method of meditation taught in The Druidry Handbook. At least five minutes should be allotted for meditation, and as much more as circumstances will permit and as will benefit those in attendance. When the meditation is finished, rise and return to the north side of the altar, facing south, and say the following words:)

I now invoke the mystery of Communion, that common unity that unites all beings throughout the worlds. All beings spring from

One; by One are they sustained, and in One do they find their rest. One the hidden glory rising through the realms of Abred; One the manifest glory rejoicing in the realms of Gwynfydd; One the unsearchable glory beyond all created being in Ceugant; and these three are resumed in One.

(Extend your hands over the altar in blessing. Say:)

From that One, through the radiant Sun and the nurturing Earth, through the powers of the elements made manifest in wind and light and rain and soil, the harvest and the vintage come forth for the sustenance of all. May the powers of the elements and the spirit of life now likewise hallow this bread and this wine, that they may be fitting vessels for the light of heaven and the life of Earth.

(Lower hands at this point. A prayer may be inserted here, calling on any deity or deities that you wish to preside over the working. Whether or not this is done, the next step is to say:)

Holy powers of living nature, may your blessing abide in this work, and radiate from it to bless the living Earth and all that lives upon her; to bless the Druid community and all who hold Nature in reverence; to bless the Ancient Order of Druids in America and all its members; and to bless all who participate here today.

(If you wish to direct the blessings of the work toward a particular person, place, or purpose, go on to say the following: May your blessing extend especially to (name), and if appropriate, describe the situation that you feel needs the blessing of the powers. Whether or not this is done, proceed to say:)

In the presence of the One, with the help of the powers, let the mystery of Communion be made manifest in space and time, in this place, in this time.

(Lift paten from atop chalice with left hand, and with right, move chalice to the right side of the altar. Place paten with bread in the center of the altar. Take the bread in both hands, raise it silently in offering, and then replace it on the paten. Say:)

I invoke Spirit Below.

(If you wish, you may say instead In the name of (Deity), I invoke Spirit Below, calling upon whatever deity you wish to invoke in relation to the telluric current. In either case, proceed to say the following:)

Power of the deeps, holy mystery in the Earth's heart, receive this offering! As the grain rises from the buried seed of winter to flower and fulfill the circle of its being, so let a ray of the telluric current arise and fill this bread with the power and blessing and grace of the Earth.

(Pause at this point, and visualize a ray of green light rising from the heart of the Earth, through the altar and paten, into the bread. Make this visualization as clear and intense as possible. Then say:)

The telluric current has arisen.

(Next, take the cruets, and pour water and wine into the chalice. Set the cruets aside. Take the chalice in both hands and raise it in offering high above the center of the altar. Say:)

I invoke Spirit Above.

(If you wish, you may say instead In the name of (Deity), I invoke Spirit Above, calling upon whatever deity you wish to invoke in relation to the solar current. In either case, proceed to say the following:)

Power of the heights, holy mystery in the sun's heart, receive this offering! As the radiance of summer shines upon the grape to ripen and renew the circle of its being, so let a ray of the solar current descend and fill this wine with the power and blessing and grace of the Sun.

(Pause at this point, and visualize a ray of golden light descending from the heart of the Sun into the cup and the wine. Make this visualization as clear and intense as possible. Then say:)

The solar current has descended.
> *(Lower chalice and hold in right hand. Take bread from paten with left hand, and raise it above the chalice. Say:)*

From above to below, from below to above, the two currents are awakened. In their union—
> *(As you continue with the words below, dip the bread into the wine. Visualize a sphere of brilliant, pure white light, like a full moon, taking shape around the chalice as the bread and wine come into contact.)*

—the union of Sun and Earth, let the lunar current be born, the wondrous child and jewel of light. Let its radiance extend to all beings, that the land may be blessed to fruitfulness and that all who seek Gwynfydd shall attain it.
> *(Take the bread from the wine and partake of it. If anyone else is present and wishes to partake of the communion, place a piece of bread in their hands and then hold the chalice so that they may dip the bread in it, and partake. When all who wish to partake of the communion have done so, place the chalice on the empty paten and proceed to the meditation and closing.)*

After the Communion ceremony is completed, the celebrant and all others present should devote at least a short additional time to meditation, this time simply focusing wordless attention on the ceremony itself and any experiences they may have had during it. Once the meditation is finished, the Grove should be closed by way of the ceremony given earlier.

The one additional action to be performed after a Communion ceremony is that, when the excess power left over from the working is returned to the Earth for her blessing, the wine remaining in the cup is poured out onto the Earth, if the ceremony has been performed outdoors, or into a bowl or cauldron at the foot of the altar, if the ceremony has been performed indoors. In the latter case, after the ceremony is finished, the celebrant should take the bowl or cauldron to a place where the wine may be poured out directly upon the Earth. In either case the celebrant should say, as he or she pours the libation upon the ground, "May the holy powers receive this offering."

The chalice, paten, and cruets should be rinsed with clean running water after they are used in the Communion ceremony, and the rinse water poured out upon the Earth; the vessels are then washed in the ordinary way. If the ceremony is performed indoors and the extra wine has been poured into a bowl or cauldron, the rinse water may be added to it, and poured out onto the Earth along with it.

The Gnostic Celtic Church

Seasonal Celebrations

Each of the world's religious traditions has a pattern of celebrations spread around the cycle of the seasons, and Druidry is no exception. From the early days of the Druid Revival, when antiquarians noted the orientation of such ancient sites as Stonehenge to the sun's positions at the solstices and equinoxes, these four points around the wheel of the year have been the great celebrations and feasts of modern Druids, and they remain the common festivals in most of today's Druid orders.

A great many people outside the Druid community, and a smaller number of people within it, assume that the eight festivals of the modern Neopagan movement are, or ought to be, kept by Druids. Despite claims of great antiquity made for it, though, the "eightfold year-wheel" is a modern invention. It was devised in the early 1950s by Gerald Gardner, the founder of modern Wicca, and Ross Nichols, an influential figure in the British Druid community. The ingredients they used for their creation were old—the solstices and equinoxes from the Druid Revival, and a set of four Irish festivals, founded in certain old sources, that fall roughly halfway in between the solstices and equinoxes—but the combination was new: there is no record before the early 1950s of anyone, anywhere, celebrating those eight festivals, and only those eight festivals, as a sacred calendar.

Its modern origin does not make the eightfold Neopagan festival cycle invalid, for Druids or anyone else—every sacred calendar was new at some point in its history—and several contemporary Druid orders have adopted the eight festivals. AODA, however, is not among those. Its seasonal celebrations remain the solstices and equinoxes, though it encourages its Groves, study groups, and members to celebrate any additional festivals they wish. The Gnostic Celtic Church follows the same custom; the solstices and equinoxes are the anchors of its ritual year, though individual priests and priestesses are welcome to add any other celebrations they wish to their ritual calendar if they so choose.

The solstices and equinoxes have a special meaning in the traditions that flow into the AODA and GCC alike. As the defining points in the astronomical relationship between Sun and Earth, they are seen as critical times in the interaction of the solar and telluric currents, the two great flows of nwyfre or life force that are central to our ritual work. The equinoxes mark a change in polarity: in the northern hemisphere (matters are reversed south of the equator), at the spring equinox, the solar current is more active, while the fall equinox begins the season in which the telluric current takes the lead. The solstices mark the high point of each current's period of predominance. Thus each of these four times are suitable seasons for intensive work with the two currents, applying the tools of human imagination and will to bring the currents into contact and create the lunar current of fertility and blessing.

The four ceremonies that follow have this goal. They are closely modeled on the equinox and solstice ceremonies for AODA Groves, which may be found in The Druid Grove Handbook. They have been revised for solitary performance, and to permit the inclusion of the Communion ceremony as a final stage in the working. Priests and priestesses who do not attend the quarterly celebrations of an AODA Grove or study group are encouraged to make use of these rituals to bring their own spiritual practice into engagement with the greater cycle of the seasons.

Spring Equinox Ceremony

(The altar may be decorated with spring flowers or other decorations appropriate to the season; a yellow altar cloth may be used, by itself or over the white cloth. Three tall unlit candles are set on the altar: a green candle in the east, a white candle in the south, and a blue candle in the west. These represent the Three Rays of Light.

(The Grove is opened with the solitary Grove opening ceremony and the Sphere of Protection ritual. Once these are complete, go to the north side of the altar, facing south, and say:)

The Spring Equinox has arrived, and the Sun and Earth renew the bonds that unite them. In this time of balanced powers, let us invoke the blessings of all the holy ones upon the Grove, the order and the Earth.

In the world of nature, the winter has ended and the Sun has completed half his long journey toward the north. The streams are full of water from the melting snow and the spring rains; sap rises in the trees and flowers begin to bloom. Birds return from their winter dwellings far to the south as life wakes from its time of sleep.

The ancients knew this season as the seedtime of the year, not only for the husbandman and the herdsman but also for those who stand at the gates between the Seen and the Unseen. They recognized at this time the power of the thought held in the mind's clarity and the word spoken upon the wind's breath; they called down wisdom from the Sun and called up power from the Earth to illuminate their minds.

Therefore the work of this season begins from the quarter of Air.

(Go to the eastern quarter of the Grove and face the altar. While saying the following words, visualize the presence of the elements of Air and Water in their quarters, and feel the polarity between them.)

East; West. Air; Water. The realm of the Mind; the realm of the Heart. May they enter into the great harmony.

(Go to altar and light the green candle, then return to the east. While saying the following words, visualize the presence of the elements of Fire and Earth in their quarters, and feel the polarity between them.)

South; North. Fire; Earth. The realm of the Spirit; the realm of the Body. May they enter into the great harmony.

(Go to altar and light the white candle, then return to the east. While saying the following words, visualize the presence of all four elements in their quarters, and feel the complex fourfold relationship among them.)

The realm of the Winds; the realm of the Flames; the realm of the Waves; the realm of the Stones. May they enter into the great harmony.

(Go to altar and light the blue candle, then take the cauldron of incense and return to the east, facing eastwards, holding up the cauldron, as though in offering.)

By the hawk of May in the heights of morning, I invoke the air and the spirits of the air! May their blessings be with the living Earth during the season to come.

(Imagine a blazing star at the zenith, almost infinitely far above the Grove; this is Fomalhaut, the Royal Star governing the ceremony. When this image is well established, take the incense cauldron back to the altar and replace it, and then take the cauldron of fire and go to the south. Face southwards and hold up the cauldron, as though in offering.)

By the white stag of the summer greenwood, I invoke the fire and the spirits of the fire! May their blessings be with the living Earth during the season to come.

(Imagine a ray of light descending from the star at infinite height to the golden sphere of the Sun, blazing at zenith above the Grove, high above but much closer than the star. When this image is well established, take the cauldron of fire back to the altar, replace it, and

then take the cauldron of water and go to the west. Face westwards and hold up the cauldron, as though in offering.)

By the salmon of wisdom who dwells in the sacred pool, I invoke the water and the spirits of the water! May their blessings be with the living Earth during the season to come.

(Imagine the ray of light descending further from the blazing Sun to the sphere of the full Moon standing at zenith above the Grove, high above but much closer than the Sun. When this image is well established, take the cauldron of water back to the altar, replace it, and then take the cauldron of earth and go to the north. Face northwards and hold up the cauldron, as though in offering.)

By the great bear who guards the starry heavens, I invoke the earth and the spirits of the earth! May their blessings be with the living Earth during the season to come.

(Imagine the ray of light descending from the shining Moon all the way to the Sphere of Protection you established around the Grove. The entire Sphere is seen to be filled with rainbow-colored light, which radiates outward in all directions. When this image is well established, take the cauldron of earth back to the altar, replace it, and then return to the north of the altar, facing south. Say:)

In this season of spring may the Sun send forth his rays of blessing; may the Earth receive that blessing and bring forth her abundance.

(Be seated. Open the Lection text, and say:)

The Lection for this ceremony is from *(name of book or other source).*
(At this point read the text aloud. The text should be chosen to correspond with the season. When it is done, set the text aside, and enter into meditation. When the meditation is finished, say:)

May the holy powers enlighten my mind *(or: our minds).*
(Rise and return to the north side of the altar, facing south, and say the following words:)

In this sacred time of balanced powers, in this sacred space in the midst of the elements, I invoke the mystery of Communion...

(At this point the Communion ceremony is performed in full, following on the words just spoken. When the Communion ceremony is finished, be seated and meditate on the season and the gifts it gives to all, then close the Grove in the usual way.)

Summer Solstice Ceremony

(The altar may be decorated with summer greenery or other decorations appropriate to the season, and a red altar cloth may be used, by itself or over the white cloth. Three tall unlit candles are set on the altar: a green candle in the east, a white candle in the south, and a blue candle in the west. These represent the Three Rays of Light.

(The Grove is opened with the solitary Grove opening ceremony and the Sphere of Protection ritual. Once these are complete, go to the north side of the altar, facing south, and say:)

The Summer Solstice has arrived, and the Sun and Earth manifest the polarities of being. In this time of balanced powers, let us invoke the blessings of all the holy ones upon the Grove, the order and the Earth.

In the world of nature, spring's promise has given way to summer's fulfillment and the Sun now stands at his highest point in the sky, preparing for his long journey into darkness. The land is mantled in green as every growing thing bends its strength toward the harvest. Life rejoices in the golden afternoon of the year even as it makes its preparations for the cold months to come.

The ancients knew this season as the year's bright summit, and waited in their stone circles for the fiery sign of midsummer sunrise, the seal of harmony that unites the turning worlds. They recognized at this time the power of destiny born from the innermost self and the kindling flame of the awakening spirit; they turned their faces to the Sun and set their feet upon the Earth to accomplish the work of their wills.

Therefore the work of this season begins from the quarter of Fire.

(Go to the southern quarter of the Grove and face the altar. While saying the following words, visualize the presence of the elements of Fire and Earth in their quarters, and feel the polarity between them.)

South; North. Fire; Earth. The realm of the Spirit; the realm of the Body. May they enter into the great harmony.

(Go to altar and light the green candle, then return to the south. While saying the following words, visualize the presence of the elements of Air and Water in their quarters, and feel the polarity between them.)

East; West. Air; Water. The realm of the Mind; the realm of the Heart: May they enter into the great harmony.

(Go to altar and light the white candle, then return to the south. While saying the following words, visualize the presence of all four elements in their quarters, and feel the complex fourfold relationship among them.)

The realm of the Flames; the realm of the Waves; the realm of the Stones; the realm of the Winds. May they enter into the great harmony.

(Go to altar and light the blue candle, then take the cauldron of incense and go to the east, facing eastwards, holding up the cauldron, as though in offering.)

By the hawk of May in the heights of morning, I invoke the air and the spirits of the air! May their blessings be with the living Earth during the season to come.

(Imagine a blazing star at the zenith, almost infinitely far above the Grove; this is Aldebaran, the Royal Star governing the ceremony. When this image is well established, take the incense cauldron back to the altar and replace it, and then take the cauldron of fire and go to the south. Face southwards and hold up the cauldron, as though in offering.)

By the white stag of the summer greenwood, I invoke the fire and the spirits of the fire! May their blessings be with the living Earth during the season to come.

(Imagine a ray of light descending from the star at infinite height to the golden sphere of the Sun, blazing at zenith above the Grove,

high above but much closer than the star. When this image is well established, take the cauldron of fire back to the altar, replace it, and then take the cauldron of water and go to the west. Face westwards and hold up the cauldron, as though in offering.)

By the salmon of wisdom who dwells in the sacred pool, I invoke the water and the spirits of the water! May their blessings be with the living Earth during the season to come.

(Imagine the ray of light descending further from the blazing Sun to the sphere of the full Moon standing at zenith above the Grove, high above but much closer than the Sun. When this image is well established, take the cauldron of water back to the altar, replace it, and then take the cauldron of earth and go to the north. Face northwards and hold up the cauldron, as though in offering.)

By the great bear who guards the starry heavens, I invoke the earth and the spirits of the earth! May their blessings be with the living Earth during the season to come.

(Imagine the ray of light descending from the shining Moon all the way to the Sphere of Protection you established around the Grove. The entire Sphere is seen to be filled with rainbow-colored light, which radiates outward in all directions. When this image is well established, take the cauldron of earth back to the altar, replace it, and then return to the north of the altar, facing south. Say:)

In this season of summer may the Sun make manifest the mystery of Light. May the Earth reflect that manifestation in the mystery of Life.

(Be seated. Open the Lection text, and say:)

The Lection for this ceremony is from (name of book or other source).

(At this point read the text aloud. The text should be chosen to correspond with the season. When it is done, set the text aside, and enter into meditation. When the meditation is finished, say:)

May the holy powers enlighten my mind (or: our minds).

(Rise and return to the north side of the altar, facing south, and say the following words:)

In this sacred time of balanced powers, in this sacred space in the midst of the elements, I invoke the mystery of Communion...

(At this point the Communion ceremony is performed in full, following on the words just spoken. When the Communion ceremony is finished, be seated and meditate on the season and the gifts it gives to all, then close the Grove in the usual way.)

Autumn Equinox Ceremony

(The altar may be decorated with autumn leaves and fruit or other decorations appropriate to the season, and a blue altar cloth may be used, by itself or over the white cloth. Three tall unlit candles are set on the altar: a green candle in the east, a white candle in the south, and a blue candle in the west. These represent the Three Rays of Light.

(The Grove is opened with the solitary Grove opening ceremony and the Sphere of Protection ritual. Once these are complete, go to the north side of the altar, facing south, and say:)

The Autumn Equinox has arrived, and the Sun and Earth renew the bonds that unite them. In this time of balanced powers, let us invoke the blessings of all the holy ones upon the Grove, the order and the Earth.

In the world of nature, summer has given way and the Sun has descended from the heights of heaven into the south. The leaves of the trees blaze with orange and red as the fields turn harvest gold. The cries of the geese sound overhead as they begin their long journey toward their winter homes. Squirrels leap from branch to branch as they prepare for the long cold months to come; the sound of clashing antlers rings through the woods as stags test their strength before the watchful eyes of does.

The ancients knew this season as the harvest time of the year, not only for those who gathered in the sheaves and led the cattle down from summer pastures but also for the wise whose harvest is the lore of past ages and the whispers of the Unseen. They recognized at this time the power of the desire cherished in the heart's silence and the bonds that reach from person to person like the sea uniting shore with shore; they called down power from the Sun and called up wisdom from the Earth to illuminate their hearts.

Therefore the work of this season begins from the quarter of Water.

(Go to the western quarter of the Grove and face the altar. While saying the following words, visualize the presence of the elements of Water and Air in their quarters, and feel the polarity between them.)

West; East. Water; Air. The realm of the Heart; the realm of the Mind. May they enter into the great harmony.

(Go to altar and light the green candle, then return to the west. While saying the following words, visualize the presence of the elements of Earth and Fire in their quarters, and feel the polarity between them.)

North; South. Earth; Fire. The realm of the Body; the realm of the Spirit. May they enter into the great harmony.

(Go to altar and light the white candle, then return to the west. While saying the following words, visualize the presence of all four elements in their quarters, and feel the complex fourfold relationship among them.)

The realm of the Waves; the realm of the Stones; the realm of the Winds; the realm of the Flames. May they enter into the great harmony.

(Go to altar and light the blue candle, then take the cauldron of incense and go to the east, facing eastwards, holding up the cauldron, as though in offering.)

By the hawk of May in the heights of morning, I invoke the air and the spirits of the air! May their blessings be with the living Earth during the season to come.

(Imagine a blazing star at the zenith, almost infinitely far above the Grove; this is Regulus, the Royal Star governing the ceremony. When this image is well established, take the incense cauldron back to the altar and replace it, and then take the cauldron of fire and go to the south. Face southwards and hold up the cauldron, as though in offering.)

By the white stag of the summer greenwood, I invoke the fire and the spirits of the fire! May their blessings be with the living Earth during the season to come.

(Imagine a ray of light descending from the star at infinite height to the golden sphere of the Sun, blazing at zenith above the Grove, high above but much closer than the star. When this image is well established, take the cauldron of fire back to the altar, replace it, and then take the cauldron of water and go to the west. Face westwards and hold up the cauldron, as though in offering.)

By the salmon of wisdom who dwells in the sacred pool, I invoke the water and the spirits of the water! May their blessings be with the living Earth during the season to come.

(Imagine the ray of light descending further from the blazing Sun to the sphere of the full Moon standing at zenith above the Grove, high above but much closer than the Sun. When this image is well established, take the cauldron of water back to the altar, replace it, and then take the cauldron of earth and go to the north. Face northwards and hold up the cauldron, as though in offering.)

By the great bear who guards the starry heavens, I invoke the earth and the spirits of the earth! May their blessings be with the living Earth during the season to come.

(Imagine the ray of light descending from the shining Moon all the way to the Sphere of Protection you established around the Grove. The entire Sphere is seen to be filled with rainbow-colored light, which radiates outward in all directions. When this image is well established, take the cauldron of earth back to the altar, replace it, and then return to the north of the altar, facing south. Say:)

In this season of autumn may the Sun send forth his rays of blessing; may the Earth receive that blessing and bring forth her abundance.

(Be seated. Open the Lection text, and say:)

The Lection for this ceremony is from (name of book or other source).

(At this point read the text aloud. The text should be chosen to correspond with the season. When it is done, set the text aside, and enter into meditation. When the meditation is finished, say:)

May the holy powers enlighten my mind (or: our minds).

(Rise and return to the north side of the altar, facing south, and say the following words:)

In this sacred time of balanced powers, in this sacred space in the midst of the elements, I invoke the mystery of Communion...

(At this point the Communion ceremony is performed in full, following on the words just spoken. When the Communion ceremony is finished, be seated and meditate on the season and the gifts it gives to all, then close the Grove in the usual way.)

Winter Solstice Ceremony

(The altar may be decorated with winter evergreens or other decorations appropriate to the season, and a green altar cloth may be used, by itself or over the white cloth. Three tall unlit candles are set on the altar: a green candle in the east, a white candle in the south, and a blue candle in the west. These represent the Three Rays of Light.

(The Grove is opened with the solitary Grove opening ceremony and the Sphere of Protection ritual. Once these are complete, go to the north side of the altar, facing south, and say:)

The Winter Solstice has arrived, and the Sun and Earth manifest the polarities of being. In this time of balanced powers, let us invoke the blessings of all the holy ones upon the Grove, the order and the Earth.

In the world of nature, the harvest is over and the Sun has descended to the place of his death and rebirth. Cold blows the wind, and colder still lie the snow and the bare earth and the bare black branches of the trees beneath the bright stars; ice rimes the edges of the streams and breath bursts white from the lips. Only those creatures that cannot sleep the winter away pace through the silence of the winter days and wait for the coming of spring.

The ancients knew this season as the end and beginning of the year, and waited in their stone circles for the first light of the newborn sun, the promise of the new year yet to come. They recognized at this time the power of patience and the wisdom of the world beneath the turning stars, the lessons woven by countless seasons into bone and sinew and sense; they gazed with renewed wonder on the pale Sun and the cold Earth as they awaited the common destiny of all material things

Therefore the work of this season begins from the quarter of Earth.

(Go to the northern quarter of the Grove and face the altar. While saying the following words, visualize the presence of the elements of Earth and Fire in their quarters, and feel the polarity between them.)

North; South. Earth; Fire. The realm of the Body; the realm of the Spirit. May they enter into the great harmony.

(Go to altar and light the green candle, then return to the north. While saying the following words, visualize the presence of the elements of Water and Air in their quarters, and feel the polarity between them.)

West; East. Water; Air. The realm of the Heart; the realm of the Mind. May they enter into the great harmony.

(Go to altar and light the white candle, then return to the north. While saying the following words, visualize the presence of all four elements in their quarters, and feel the complex fourfold relationship among them.)

The realm of the Stones; the realm of the Winds; the realm of the Flames; the realm of the Waves. May they enter into the great harmony.

(Go to altar and light the blue candle, then take the cauldron of incense and go to the east, facing eastwards, holding up the cauldron, as though in offering.)

By the hawk of May in the heights of morning, I invoke the air and the spirits of the air! May their blessings be with the living Earth during the season to come.

(Imagine a blazing star at the zenith, almost infinitely far above the Grove; this is Antares, the Royal Star governing the ceremony. When this image is well established, take the incense cauldron back to the altar and replace it, and then take the cauldron of fire and go to the south. Face southwards and hold up the cauldron, as though in offering.)

By the white stag of the summer greenwood, I invoke the fire and the spirits of the fire! May their blessings be with the living Earth during the season to come.

(Imagine a ray of light descending from the star at infinite height to the golden sphere of the Sun, blazing at zenith above the Grove,

high above but much closer than the star. When this image is well established, take the cauldron of fire back to the altar, replace it, and then take the cauldron of water and go to the west. Face westwards and hold up the cauldron, as though in offering.)

By the salmon of wisdom who dwells in the sacred pool, I invoke the water and the spirits of the water! May their blessings be with the living Earth during the season to come.

(Imagine the ray of light descending further from the blazing Sun to the sphere of the full Moon standing at zenith above the Grove, high above but much closer than the Sun. When this image is well established, take the cauldron of water back to the altar, replace it, and then take the cauldron of earth and go to the north. Face northwards and hold up the cauldron, as though in offering.)

By the great bear who guards the starry heavens, I invoke the earth and the spirits of the earth! May their blessings be with the living Earth during the season to come.

(Imagine the ray of light descending from the shining Moon all the way to the Sphere of Protection you established around the Grove. The entire Sphere is seen to be filled with rainbow-colored light, which radiates outward in all directions. When this image is well established, take the cauldron of earth back to the altar, replace it, and then return to the north of the altar, facing south. Say:)

In this season of winter may the Sun make manifest the mystery of Light. May the Earth reflect that manifestation in the mystery of Life.

(Be seated. Open the Lection text, and say:)

The Lection for this ceremony is from (name of book or other source).

(At this point read the text aloud. The text should be chosen to correspond with the season. When it is done, set the text aside, and enter into meditation. When the meditation is finished, say:)

May the holy powers enlighten my mind (or: our minds).

(Rise and return to the north side of the altar, facing south, and say the following words:)

In this sacred time of balanced powers, in this sacred space in the midst of the elements, I invoke the mystery of Communion...

(At this point the Communion ceremony is performed in full, following on the words just spoken. When the Communion ceremony is finished, be seated and meditate on the season and the gifts it gives to all, then close the Grove in the usual way.)

Spiritual Practices

The deacons, priests and priestesses, and bishops of the Gnostic Celtic Church have the duty and the privilege of creating personal spiritual practices to deepen and enrich their own experience of the Gnosis of Nature. Three specific practices are also assigned to deacons as part of their training for ordination, and these are given below. They may be retained, transformed, or replaced by the individual ordinand as he or she develops an individual path, whether or not that path leads to ordination and consecration in the other holy orders of the GCC.

The Home Altar

Many faiths around the world teach the practice of establishing a sacred place within the home. Most Japanese homes, for example, have a kamidana, a small shelf in a place of honor where offerings of rice, sake, salt, and water are given to the kami, the deities of the Shinto faith. Two thousand years ago, nearly all Roman houses contained a similar shrine where comparable offerings were made to the lares and penates, the household guardian deities of Roman pagan religion. Elsewhere around the world and across the centuries, the same custom has given rise to household shrines of many types.

This custom has much to offer the work of the Hermitage of the Heart. Setting aside some small corner of the home, be it a shelf, the top of a dresser or other piece of furniture, or a purpose-built shrine, provides a physical representation of the presence of the holy powers the practitioner reveres, and the everyday process of tending the home altar helps keep the mind oriented toward the entities and ideals that the altar and its furnishings symbolize. Each deacon of the GCC is thus requested to establish such an altar and tend it daily, at least during the period between reception as a deacon and ordination as a priest or priestess.

The exact form and furnishings of the home altar will vary depending on personal tastes, and on how individual practitioners conceptualize the holy powers whose presence and blessing they seek to invoke into their lives and homes. One simple and suitable form of altar is a flat surface perhaps two feet wide and one foot deep. It may be covered by an altar cloth, which may be white, or some other color that has symbolic meaning for the practitioner; altar cloths that change with the seasons, like the cloths used in the seasonal rituals, are also a suitable choice.

Other altar decorations are equally a matter of the individual deacon's choice. Two candles in candlesticks, for example, may be placed on the altar, one at each side toward the back of the altar, to represent the polarities of being. A censer (incense burner) may be placed toward the center of the altar front, unless health or other reasons make it inadvisable to use incense. Offering bowls for any other offerings you wish to make—for example, a bowl of clear water and a bowl of salt—may be put to either side of the censer, or at the altar front in its absence.

Another common furnishing for the home altar consists of one or more images to represent the holy powers of nature. These will inevitably vary depending on the personal Awen and religious ideas of the individual. Those who experience the powers as personal gods and goddesses may wish to acquire statues or pictures of the deities they revere, and place these at the center back of the altar, behind the censer and offerings. Those who experience the powers in more impersonal forms may prefer to find some more abstract symbol to represent the focus of their reverence, and use that instead.

Altar cloth, candles, censer, and one or more images may be considered a good basic set of furnishings for a home altar, though this is merely a suggestion, not a mandatory form. How elaborate the altar and its furnishings become is wholly up to the individual, though in most cases clutter is not an advantage.

The home altar should be tended at least once a day. Tending the altar includes such actions as lighting candles, burning some incense, changing offerings if they are no longer fresh—for example, an offering of clear water should be changed daily, and an offering of salt should be changed when the first sign of discoloration appears—and removing any dust or the like. It is usually most convenient to combine this with the practice of morning prayer. For reasons of safety, candles and incense should never be left to burn unattended.

Morning Prayer

Prayer is another practice common to religious, spiritual, and mystical traditions around the world. It is important not to mistake prayer as a whole for the debased form that has become popular in some modern religious traditions, in which it too often becomes a matter of begging a god for favors—"and bids me, at my Father's throne, make all my wants and wishes known," in the words of a well-known Protestant hymn. The practice of communing verbally with spiritual realities has much more to offer than this.

The philosopher Martin Buber pointed out many years ago that human beings relate to other beings, broadly speaking, in two ways, which he termed "I-it" and "I-Thou" relationships. I-it relationships are instrumental in nature: the I, the conscious self, uses something outside itself as an instrument to carry out its intentions. I-Thou relationships, by contrast, are interactive: the I relates to something outside itself not as an instrument of its intention but as another self, a Thou, with intentions of its own.

Both modes of relationship have their proper functions in human life. One of the pathologies of modern society, however, is a pervasive replacement of I-Thou by I-it relationships, and thus the abandonment of interaction in favor of instrumental manipulation. This may be seen often enough in human relationships, but its impacts on the relationships that link humanity to the nonhuman cosmos are even more destructive. The core delusion of modernity might even be summed up as the notion that it is a good idea to treat the rest of the universe as no more than an instrument of human intentions.

It is among the central themes of spiritual traditions from around the world and across the centuries that a purely instrumental approach to the cosmos is unbalanced and ultimately destructive to the whole range of human and ecological values, and thus needs to be balanced by appropriate efforts to maintain an interactive, I-Thou relationship with the cosmos and the spiritual powers that guide and shape it. Prayer is a core element of this work. Human beings, whatever else they are or may become, are richly communicative social primates, and thus one of the simplest and most effective ways for most human beings to enter into an I-Thou relationship with anyone and anything in the universe of human experience is to talk with it.

Those who experience the divine in personal form, as one or more deities, have an advantage here, but prayer also plays a lively and important part in many traditions that understand the divine in impersonal forms. Each deacon of the GCC is therefore requested to set aside time each morning, preferably before any other activity, to pray to the holy powers of Nature, addressing them in whatever form or manifestation he or she finds most meaningful.

The most basic form of prayer in the Druid Revival tradition is the well-known Universal Druid Prayer. In its standard AODA form—there are a number of different versions, going back at least to the 18th century—it reads:

Grant, O holy ones, thy protection;
And in protection, strength;
And in strength, understanding;
And in understanding, knowledge;
And in knowledge, the knowledge of justice;
And in the knowledge of justice, the love of it;
And in that love, the love of all existences;
And in the love of all existences, the love of Earth our mother
and all goodness.

Repeating this prayer each morning before the home altar may be considered a reasonable minimum, provided that time is taken to think through what the prayer means, rather than simply reciting it from memory. More generally, this same point should be kept in mind with all prayer: it is only an effective means of spiritual practice if you know what you are saying, and mean it.

The rote repetition of a set of words that are neither understood nor meant is no more effective when directed toward spiritual realities than it would be, for example, when directed toward another human being in a close relationship. It is worth noting that even in those traditions that use mantras or some close equivalent, close meditation on the meaning and symbolism of the mantra is an important part of the practice—Hindu and Buddhist texts, for example, go into immense detail concerning the meaning of the sacred syllable Aum.

Most people will accordingly find that the practice of morning prayer benefits from a more personal phrasing, either instead of established formal prayers or alongside them. For an example of the latter, addressing the holy powers of Nature in an extempore fashion, saying whatever might be most appropriate and relevant at that time, might be followed by a deliberate and thoughtful repetition of the Universal Druid Prayer.

Whatever the approach chosen, however, the daily practice of prayer—of establishing an I-Thou relationship with the holy powers of Nature through the most natural human means of relating to another being—has important lessons to teach. Deacons of the GCC, and any others who choose to practice the spiritual disciplines outlined on these pages, will find that the practice of prayer itself will quickly become their best teacher.

Evening Lection

The third practice assigned to deacons who are training for ordination as priests or priestesses in the GCC is the habit of lection, that is, of attentive reading of appropriate texts as a deliberate spiritual practice. The practice of lection has already been mentioned above as part of the Communion ceremony, but it can and should also be pursued in its own right.

Reading can be done in many different ways, ranging from the most superficial skimming to the kind of close reading in which a text is examined one word at a time, and squeezed for every drop of meaning it contains. The practice of lection traditionally lies between these two extremes, though it is noticeably closer to the latter of them. Lection is reflective reading—a process of reading in which the thoughts and responses of the reader are as important as the words of the text.

The practice of lection begins with the selection of a short text—in most cases, between a paragraph and a page—on any subject the practitioner finds suitable. As with the lections that are part of the Communion ceremony, books of spiritual philosophy, ecological wisdom, nature poetry, or observations of nature are recommended as sources for the evening lections of Deacons, but each person will soon discover through practice what texts best reflect the call of his or her own Awen.

When the time of daily lection arrives, the practitioner sits down in a comfortable position—the standard posture of meditation may or may not be used here, depending on individual preference— and reads the selected text. This reading may be done silently or in a low voice, again depending on individual preference, and should be done slowly enough to allow the reader to pay attention to his or her own immediate responses to the text as it proceeds. Once the reading is finished, a period of silent reflection follows. This need not be as structured as formal discursive meditation; the goal is simply for the practitioner to consider the text and his or her responses to it, and to allow any insights to surface that might come in response to either of these.

Lection can be practiced at any convenient time of day or night, but deacons in training for the priesthood or priestesshood are encouraged to practice it at the end of the day, just before retiring for the night. The last thoughts before sleep have a subtle but powerful influence on the workings of the sleeping mind, and through this on the broader state of consciousness. "Tuning in" the mind to the ways of spirit and the patterns of nature immediately before sleep thus gently reorients consciousness away from the chatter that normally fills it, and helps it center itself ever more fully on the deeper realities of existence.

Requirements for Ordination

While anyone who desires to do so may pursue a path of service and devotion of the kind the Gnostic Celtic Church offers its members, participation in the holy orders of the GCC is not suited to everyone. Those who wish to take up the Rule of Awen and follow the path of the Hermitage of the Heart need to accept and fulfill certain requirements, which include but are not limited to those of the standard AODA study program.

There is no requirement for members of the GCC to pass through all three of the holy orders. Just as a member of AODA may choose to remain in the Candidate grade, or to advance from there through the study program to the First, Second, or Third Degrees, a member of AODA who wishes to pursue a way of nature spirituality in the deeper and more personal form offered by the GCC may choose to be received as a deacon but proceed no further, or may choose to do the necessary work and be ordained as a priest or priestess and proceed no further, or may in due time be consecrated as a bishop. The requirements for each of these stages are listed below.

Reception, ordination, or consecration in the GCC is limited to members of AODA, however, and depends in part on the fulfillment of the requirements of the AODA study program. It is not a replacement for AODA's system of Druid training, but a supplement and an intensification of that training, and it does not grant any rights or privileges within AODA apart from those inherent in the degrees of the Order. Nor, it must always be remembered, does any level of participation in the life and work of the GCC justify claiming authority over any other person, in or out of the GCC or AODA.

The Gnostic Celtic Church

Requirements for Deacons

The order of deacon is primarily intended to serve as an introductory stage for those who wish to proceed to the priesthood or priestesshood, though it may also provide a valid framework for those who wish to work with some of the spiritual disciplines of the GCC but do not wish to practice the Communion ceremony on a regular basis. Members of AODA who desire reception as a deacon may receive it upon fulfilling the following requirements:

1. Completion of the AODA First Degree training program, or an appropriate program in another Druid order that has been approved for transfer credit by the Grand Grove, and initiation into the First Degree of AODA. (Candidates who qualify for the order of deacon by way of transfer credit may be required to undertake additional studies and practices, during their training for the priestly order, to ensure they have an adequate background in AODA's rituals and practices.)
2. Performance of a vigil of at least six uninterrupted hours of prayer and contemplation, seeking insight and guidance for the path toward ordination into the priestly order, after which a detailed description of the vigil and its results should be written up and submitted to the Grand Grove.
3. Submission, along with the vigil account, of a letter of intent to the Grand Grove requesting reception as a deacon.
4. Satisfactory completion of a process of reflection and conversation that explores in detail why the applicant wishes to become a deacon in the GCC and what goals he or she wishes to pursue through this work.

Reception as a deacon can be received in person from a GCC bishop, but it can also be conferred at a distance by means of a specific ritual formula in which a suitable token is blessed by a bishop and returned to the candidate for reception. Please contact the GCC for details of this process.

Requirements for Priests or Priestesses

The order of priest or priestess is the working heart of the GCC, and brings with it the responsibility to practice the Communion working, the core practice of the GCC, as a regular personal devotion. As already mentioned, the priests and priestesses of the GCC are regular rather than secular clergy. They may, if they so wish and others wish them to do so, engage in work with a congregation or the celebration of rites of passage, but their primary commitment is to personal spiritual practice and following the Rule of Awen, along the lines outlined in this book. They are in no way required to function in the capacity of clergy for any other person unless they consider themselves specifically called to that work. Any member of AODA who desires ordination as a priest or priestess may receive it upon fulfilling the following requirements:

1. Completion of the AODA Second Degree training program, or an appropriate program in another Druid order that has been approved for transfer credit by the Grand Grove. (Candidates who qualify for the priestly order by way of transfer credit may be required to undertake additional studies and practices during their training, to ensure they have an adequate background in AODA's rituals and practices.)
2. Previous ordination as a deacon in the GCC.
3. Close study of three books in addition to the seven books required for the Second Degree core curriculum. The books are as follows:
    a. *The Varieties of Religious Experience* by William James;
    b. *The Many Paths of the Independent Sacramental Tradition* by John Plummer;
    c. *The Gnostic Celtic Church: A Manual and Book of Liturgy* edited by John Michael Greer.
4. Creation of a home altar and daily practice of morning prayer and evening lection, following the framework provided in this book.
5. Regular and thorough practice of the AODA solitary Grove

ritual, Sphere of Protection ceremony, and Communion ceremony, in preparation for ordination to the priesthood.

6. An ongoing process of mentoring and discernment, to assist the future priest or priestess in developing a personal vocation and priestly practice.

Ordination as a Priest or Priestess must be received in person from a GCC Bishop; it cannot be conferred by mail or at a distance. It will normally be preceded by a vigil.

Requirements for Bishops

The order of bishop comprises those participants in the GCC who pursue their vocation to the point of embodying the entire GCC and AODA tradition in their own lives. It is not a springboard from which to pursue some other religious direction; it is specific to those who have found their spiritual home in the GCC and AODA, and wish to assist others in the work of the church and the order. For this reason the ability to confer reception, ordination, and consecration into the holy orders of the GCC is reserved to bishops. Any member of AODA who desires consecration as a bishop may receive it upon fulfilling the following requirements:

1. Completion of the AODA Third Degree training program, and initiation into the Third Degree of AODA.
2. Previous ordination as a priest or priestess in the GCC.
3. Design and completion of an extensive course of personal study, building on the foundations of the study program assigned for priests and priestesses in the GCC, which must be approved by the presiding archbishops of the GCC in advance.
4. Development of a continuing and intensive personal spiritual practice as an expression of priestly vocation, and the composition of a detailed written account of this practice.
5. A further process of mentoring and discernment to help the future bishop enrich his or her personal vocation and priestly practice.
6. A final vote of approval for consecration by the Grand Grove.

Consecration as a bishop must be received in person from at least one, and preferably three, GCC bishops; it cannot be conferred by mail or at a distance. It will normally be preceded by an extended vigil.

Rituals of Ordination

The ordination rituals of the Gnostic Celtic Church are the ceremonial forms by which those who feel called to the work of regular clergy in the GCC under the Rule of Awen formalize their commitment to that path. Each of these rituals has its own title—reception for deacons, ordination for priests and priestesses, and consecration for bishops—which are partly dictated by tradition, and partly a reflection of the different roles of the three holy orders.

In a broader sense, however, the term "ordination" applies to all three, for entering into the priesthood or priestesshood is at the core of the entire process. Deacons are essentially priests or priestesses in training; bishops, in turn, are simply experienced priests or priestesses who have made a specific commitment to the work and way of the Gnostic Celtic Church and are therefore empowered to ordain others. In a very real sense, the work of the priestly order is the work of the GCC, and the other holy orders exist to support that work.

It deserves repetition here that these rituals confer no authority over other people, within or beyond the GCC, in matters of faith and morals or any other context. To be received, ordained, or consecrated to the holy orders in the GCC is to embrace solemn responsibilities, not to assume rights or privileges. To pass through these rituals is not to be raised to a position of power over other human beings, but rather to accept the role of a servant in the Hermitage of the Heart and a follower of the Rule of Awen.

The responsibilities and duties that unfold from this commitment are not specified by the text of the rituals or the teachings of the GCC, because they will necessarily differ from one person to another. They are nonetheless serious and real, and ample time for reflection should be taken before undertaking them. It is for this reason that a vigil is part of the process of each stage of ordination.

The Vigil

Before potential candidates for reception may apply to the Grand Grove for admission to the order of deacon, as mentioned above, they are expected to complete a vigil of at least six uninterrupted hours of prayer and contemplation, seeking insight and guidance for the path toward ordination into the priestly order. Most of the details of the vigil are left up to the choice of the individual candidate; thus, for example, one candidate might choose to perform her vigil in an isolated spot in the forest during the daytime hours, while another might find it more appropriate or more practical to perform his vigil indoors at night.

The following principles, however, should be considered mandatory, unless some overriding reason such as a medical condition makes it necessary to change them; in such a case, permission must be requested and received from the Grand Grove before the vigil is performed.

1. The purpose of the vigil is to step outside the ordinary round of social interactions to prepare for the serious step of receiving holy orders. Each candidate shall therefore spend the entire vigil alone, and the place and time of the vigil shall be chosen to minimize the chance of accidental encounters with other people.

2. For the same reason, the candidate shall not use electronic communications media of any kind during the vigil, and if at all possible, such devices should not be present in the place of the vigil.

3. The vigil should be devoted to those activities central to the training and work of a deacon—that is to say, prayer, meditation, ritual, study, and serious reflection. The candidate may choose to perform ritual work during the vigil, or to mark its beginning and end. Books relevant to the candidate's personal vision of the priestly work may be brought to the place of the vigil in physical or electronic form, so that they may be read and studied, if the candidate so chooses. Should the

candidate intend his or her priestly work to take a distinctive form—for example, involving one of the arts—activities relevant to that form may also be included in the vigil.

4. Eating and drinking should only take place during the vigil if required by the candidate's physical needs, or in the ceremony of Communion, if this ceremony is performed as part of the vigil.

5. The use of alcohol during the vigil is prohibited, except in the very small amounts used in the ceremony of Communion, if this ceremony is performed as part of the vigil. No other drug may be used at all unless required by a physician's prescription.

As soon as possible after the vigil is completed, a detailed account of it, including the candidate's reflections on what he or she learned through the vigil, should be prepared. This should be submitted to the Grand Grove, as previously mentioned, along with the letter of intent requesting reception as a deacon.

A vigil is also performed by the candidate before ordination as a priest or priestess, and before consecration as a bishop. These vigils, however, are not performed prior to requesting ordination or consecration from the Grand Grove. Instead, they should take place immediately before the ritual of ordination or consecration. The duration, setting, and activities to be performed during a vigil of this kind shall be left to the free choice of the candidate, but any variation from the principles listed above should be discussed with the Grand Grove, and with the ordaining bishop or principal consecrator, well in advance of the vigil and ceremony.

Reception of a Deacon

The ritual by which an initiate of the First Degree of AODA becomes a deacon in the GCC is termed "reception," as by it the candidate is received into the regular clergy of the GCC and introduced to its life and work.

Before the ceremony, the candidate for reception should provide himself or herself with a token—a small solid object that will be blessed by the bishop and placed on or immediately above the home altar where the deacon will perform his or her morning prayers. A small stone is traditional and well suited for this purpose, and should be recommended unless the deacon-to-be has some special reason to use an object of another kind. The bishop should be sure that the deacon-to-be understands that the token will be discarded—returned to the world of nature—at such time as the deacon either advances to the priesthood or chooses to leave the diaconate, so no object whose loss will be regretted should be used for this purpose.

The candidate should be dressed in the white robe and cord belt standard in AODA practice. The bishop who performs this ceremony shall provide himself or herself with a small bottle of anointing oil, with which the token is to be anointed.

The ritual begins with the ordinary AODA Grove Ceremony opening, either the solitary form given in this book or the full form given in The Druid Grove Handbook; in the latter case, the Grove is opened in the Candidate grade, as the ritual of reception for a deacon, like all GCC ordination ceremonies, is a public ritual to which the candidate may invite anyone he or she wishes. In addition to the ordinary furnishings of a GCC altar, the chalice, paten, cruets, bread, wine, and water needed for the Communion ceremony should be present in the Grove before the opening ceremony, though they should not be placed on the altar.

Once the opening ceremony is completed in full, the ritual of reception begins.

Bishop: The order of deacon is the most basic of the three holy orders in the Gnostic Celtic Church, and comprises the first step in commitment to the Rule of Awen and the path of the Hermitage of the Heart. The period of service to which deacons are called is a time of opportunity: a time to turn away from the pressures and demands of society, in order to attend to the voice of spirit that whispers within; a time for each candidate to consider whether or not the enduring commitment to the Gnosis of Nature that comes with ordination to the priesthood or priesthood is an appropriate choice.

Let any one present who is qualified to seek reception as a deacon, and wishes to do so, advance to the south of the altar.

(The candidate does so.)

Bishop: The traditions of our church require that certain questions be asked and answered of each candidate before the ceremony of reception can proceed. Have you completed the necessary studies and been initiated as an Apprentice in the Ancient Order of Druids in America?

(The candidate answers.)

Bishop: Have you performed the preliminary vigil expected of any candidate to this order, and seriously contemplated the solemnity of the work you propose to undertake?

(The candidate answers.)

Bishop: Have you properly requested reception as a deacon from the Grand Grove of the Ancient Order of Druids in America, and passed through the process of reflection and conversation enjoined on all candidates to this first of our holy orders?

(The candidate answers.)

Bishop: Have you provided yourself with a token as was requested of you, and do you have it with you at this time?

(The candidate answers.)

Bishop: Are you now prepared, of your own free will, to be received as a deacon in the Gnostic Celtic Church, to follow the path of the Gnosis of Nature, and to take up the quest to find and follow your own Awen wherever it may lead you?

(The candidate answers.)

Bishop: In the name of what deity or sacred power do you take so serious a step?

(The candidate answers.)

Bishop: It is well. You will therefore kneel on both your knees, place the token upon the altar before you, and silently invoke the blessing of (name of deity or sacred power) upon this ceremony and your work as a deacon hereafter. When you are finished, please say aloud, "So mote it be."

(The candidate does so.)

Bishop: You will now repeat after me. In the presence of, and speak the name of your deity or sacred power—and the holy powers of nature—and of all who witness this rite—I ask to be received—as a deacon—in the Gnostic Celtic Church.—For the duration of my diaconate—I will conform cheerfully to the regulations—study the teachings—and perform the practices—appertaining to the order of deacons—and will in all things—seek to hear and heed—the voice of Awen within me.

Bishop: *(raises hands in blessing)* And in the name of (name of deity or sacred power) and of all the holy powers of nature I receive you as a deacon in the Gnostic Celtic Church. (Bishop lowers hands.)

Bishop: The diaconate among us is a probationary order, and binds you only so long as you yourself choose. You may depart from it at any time, should your own Awen or some other incentive so direct, and you may also pass beyond it, should you complete the work of a deacon and proceed to ordination into the ranks of our priests and priestesses. Thus we anoint and bless, not you yourself, but a token that you have selected.

While you remain a deacon, your token is the link that binds you to the body and the life of the Gnostic Celtic Church. Keep it upon the altar where you perform your morning devotions. Should you ever choose to leave the diaconate, return the token to the world of nature; the link will then be broken and you will be free. Should you choose to proceed to ordination into the priesthood or priestesshood, you will likewise return your token to the world of nature, but at that time you yourself will be anointed and blessed, and the link thus made cannot be broken thereafter.

(Bishop takes anointing oil, puts some on right thumb, and traces the Three Rays of Light /|\ on the token, saying:)

With this oil of blessing, and in the name of *(name of deity or sacred power)*, I consecrate and empower this token as a living link uniting *(name of deacon)* to the body and life of the Gnostic Celtic Church. May the light that was before the worlds descend upon him (or her), and guide him *(or her)* along the winding forest paths to the portal of the temple of the Gnosis of Nature.

You may take your token now. *(Deacon does so.)*

Into those who are received as deacons among us, a seed is planted. Whether that seed shall grow to flower and bear fruit depends on the care and constancy with which it is tended. Remember this, and do not neglect the studies and practices to which you have pledged yourself before the holy powers of nature and these witnesses, for it is by diligent work at the tasks before you that you will prepare yourself for the greater work that is to come.

In commemoration of this, and to bless this occasion, I invite you and all present to participate with me in the mystery of Communion.

(The chalice, paten, and cruets are placed upon the altar at this point.)

The Communion ceremony is then performed, with the bishop as celebrant. A lection suitable for the occasion should be selected beforehand, and read at the usual point in the ceremony; the newly received deacon should be the first person after the bishop to partake of the bread and wine. Once the Communion ceremony is finished, the bishop may address the Grove, and then the closing ceremony is performed.

Ordination of a Priest or Priestess

The ritual by which a deacon in the Gnostic Celtic Church is advanced to the priesthood or priestesshood is termed "ordination," as by it the candidate publicly affirms the decision to order his or her life according to the Rule of Awen.

Before the ceremony, the candidate should provide himself or herself with a stole as a symbol or his or her priestly office. The priestly stole used in the GCC is green in color, no more than three inches wide at the back of the neck and widening slightly toward the ends; it falls to the approximate level of the knees. It may be plain or decorated, as the individual priest or priestess prefers. The stole is worn when the Communion ritual is performed, and at any other time when engaged in priestly work.

In addition to the stole, the candidate should have a strip of white cloth, two feet long and six inches wide, which is used to bind his or her hands after they have been anointed. The candidate should again be clad in a white robe and cord belt. The ordaining bishop, as in the ritual for reception of deacons, should have a small bottle of anointing oil; the hands and head of the newly ordained priest or priestess will be anointed with this in the course of the ceremony.

The ritual begins with the ordinary AODA Grove Ceremony opening, either the solitary form given in this book or the full form given in *The Druid Grove Handbook*; in the latter case, the Grove is opened in the Candidate grade, as the ritual of ordination is a public ritual to which the candidate may invite anyone he or she wishes. In addition to the ordinary furnishings of a GCC altar, the chalice, paten, cruets, bread, wine, and water needed for the Communion ceremony should be present in the Grove before the opening ceremony, though they should not be placed on the altar.

Once the opening ceremony is completed in full, the ritual of ordination begins.

Bishop: The priestly order is the most important of the holy orders conferred in the Gnostic Celtic Church. To it the order of deacon is an introduction, and from it the order of bishop derives its most important role in our tradition. The work of priests and priestesses among us is to follow the path of the Hermitage of the Heart according to the Rule of Awen, and by the practice of our ceremonies and such other spiritual disciplines as they may be called to do, to bring light, blessing and healing to the living Earth and all that lives upon her. Those who propose to take upon themselves this great responsibility are enjoined first to be received as deacons among us, to pass through the training preparatory to the priestly order, and to consider well the solemnity of the order to which they aspire, before they may be ordained as priests and priestesses among us.

Let any deacon present who is prepared to receive ordination as a priest or priestess, and now wishes to do so, advance to the south of the altar.

(The candidate does so.)

Bishop: The traditions of our church require that, before the ritual of ordination shall be performed, I remind you once more of the seriousness of the burden you propose to assume. You have, it may be, until this moment lived solely for yourself, or for those whose lives you chose to link with your own; but as a priest (or priestess) in the Gnostic Celtic Church, you are called upon to live for all. The Rule of Awen, once taken up, cannot be laid down again; from the hour of your ordination henceforth you will be responsible, not to me, nor to any official of the Gnostic Celtic Church or the Ancient Order of Druids in America, nor even to the holy powers we serve, but to the voice of the living spirit within you, and to the answering voice of your own conscience, from which there is no appeal.

By this act of ordination, the Gnostic Celtic Church confers upon you no authority in matters of faith or morals, and no right to demand obedience from others, in or outside of our church and our order. You are called instead to responsibility and to service. Recognizing this, do you still wish to proceed?

(The candidate answers.)

Bishop: The traditions of our church further require that certain questions be asked and answered of each candidate before the ceremony of ordination can proceed. Have you completed the necessary studies and been initiated as a Companion in the Ancient Order of Druids in America?

(The candidate answers.)

Bishop: Have you performed the vigil expected of a deacon who seeks advancement to this order, and seriously contemplated the solemnity of the work you propose to undertake?

(The candidate answers.)

Bishop: Have you properly requested ordination as a priest (or priestess) from the Grand Grove of the Ancient Order of Druids in America, and passed through the process of training, reflection and conversation that is enjoined on all candidates for the priesthood?

(The candidate answers.)

Bishop: Have you provided yourself with a stole as was requested of you, and do you have it with you at this time?

(The candidate answers.)

Bishop: Are you now prepared, of your own free will, to be ordained as a priest (or priestess) in the Gnostic Celtic Church, to follow the path of the Gnosis of Nature yet more fully than heretofore, and to take up the Rule of Awen for the guidance of your life from this day onward forever?

(The candidate answers.)

Bishop: In the name of what deity or sacred power do you take this most serious step?

(The candidate answers.)

Bishop: It is well. You will therefore kneel on both your knees and silently invoke the blessing of (name of deity or sacred power) upon this ceremony and your work as a priest (or priestess) hereafter. When you are finished, please say aloud, "So mote it be."

(The candidate does so.)

Bishop: You will now repeat after me. In the presence of, and speak the name of your deity or sacred power—and the holy powers of nature—and of all who witness this rite—I accept the blessing and the burden—of ordination as a priest *(or priestess)*—in the Gnostic Celtic Church—now and forever.—I will make the Rule of Awen—the guide of my life—and follow the path—of the Hermitage of the Heart—as my Awen shall direct me.—By the practice of the ceremonies—that have been confided to me—and by all other means—that my Awen shall direct—I shall endeavor to bring—light, blessing and healing—to the living Earth and all that lives upon her.

Bishop: *(raises hands in blessing)* And in the name of *(name of deity or sacred power)* and of all the holy powers of nature I ordain you as a priest *(or priestess)* in the Gnostic Celtic Church. *(Bishop places hands upon candidate's head.)* Receive now my blessing and that of the Holy Gnosis.
(Bishop pauses at this point, as long as seems appropriate, to transmit the blessing, then removes hands.)

Bishop: When you were received as a deacon among us, the anointing that sealed your reception and formed the living link uniting you to the body and life of the Gnostic Celtic Church was placed, not upon you yourself, but upon a token chosen by you. This was so that if you chose to break that link, you could do so freely by casting the token away, returning it to the world of nature. The priestly order, however, may not be cast aside in this way; the act of ordination is irrevocable, and binds you forever to the commitments you have made, and the anointing that seals your ordination is made upon your head and hands. You will therefore raise your hands with the palms up, and bow your head.
(Candidate does so. Bishop takes a few drops of oil and, using the right thumb, draws the emblems of water and earth on the left palm, and those of fire and air on the right. Bishop now bids the candidate place his hands together, palm to palm, and binds them with the white cloth.)

(Bishop takes another few drops of oil and, with the right thumb, draws a circle three times over on the crown of the candidate's head. Bishop cleans thumb with a cloth, then goes around the altar, kneels beside the candidate and whispers in the candidate's ear, communicating the priestly secret.)

Bishop: *(rises and returns to north of altar)* Receive now the stole that is the emblem of your priestly office.
(Bishop places stole about candidate's neck.)

Bishop: May the light that was before the worlds descend upon you, and guide you ever in the way of Awen. May the solar and telluric currents bless and empower you, that you may in turn bring light, blessing and healing to the living earth and all that lives upon her. In the name of (name of deity or sacred power candidate gave earlier) and of all the holy powers, arise and begin your priestly office by celebrating the mystery of Communion.
(The new priest or priestess is helped to rise and to unbind his or her hands, which may be cleaned if necessary on the white cloth.)

The Communion ceremony is then performed, with the new priest or priestess as celebrant. A lection suitable for the occasion should be selected by the candidate beforehand, and read at the usual point in the ceremony; the ordaining bishop should be the first person after the priest or priestess to partake of the bread and wine. Once the Communion ceremony is finished, the bishop may address the Grove, and then the closing ceremony is performed.

Consecration of a Bishop

The ritual by which a priest or priestess in the Gnostic Celtic Church is advanced to the order of bishop is termed "consecration," as by it the candidate takes on the high task and responsibility of embodying the Rule of Awen and the traditions of the Gnostic Celtic Church to such a degree that he or she is prepared to pass on these things to others.

While the consecration of a bishop can be performed by a single bishop, it is traditional to have three bishops present to act as consecrators, and more may participate in the ceremony if this is desired and they are available. The principal consecrator, as in the previous rituals, should have a small bottle of anointing oil, with which the head and hands of the newly consecrated bishop will be anointed.

There is no special emblem worn by bishops in the Gnostic Celtic Church; the candidate should be dressed as a priest, in white robe, cord belt, and green priestly stole. The candidate should also have a strip of white cloth, two feet long and six inches wide, which is used to bind his or her hands after they have been anointed.

The ritual begins with the ordinary AODA Grove Ceremony opening, either the solitary form given in this book or the full form given in The Druid Grove Handbook; in the latter case, the Grove is opened in the Candidate grade, as the ritual of ordination is a public ritual to which the candidate may invite anyone he or she wishes. In addition to the ordinary furnishings of a GCC altar, the chalice, paten, cruets, bread, wine, and water needed for the communion ceremony should be present in the Grove before the opening ceremony, though they should not be placed on the altar.

Once the opening ceremony is completed in full, the ritual of consecration begins.

Principal Consecrator: The order of bishop represents the completion of the holy orders of the Gnostic Celtic Church. The work of a deacon is to experience the Rule of Awen and the way of the Hermitage of the Heart, before making a lasting commitment to our work and way; the work of a priest or priestess, having made that commitment, is to follow the guidance of Awen and to bring light, blessing, and healing to the living earth and all that lives upon her. The deacon, having taken up our work for a time, may set it down again and pursue some other path in life; the priest or priestess, paying heed to the promptings of Awen, may follow its guidance along paths that lead far from our traditions and teachings.

There is however a special place for those who, having entered into the priestly order and taken up the Rule of Awen, decide after sufficient experience and due reflection that their path leads them to remain with the Ancient Order of Druids in America and the Gnostic Celtic Church, and to embrace the work of transmitting its teachings, its rites, and its degrees to those who shall come after. This is the work our traditions assign to our bishops.

Those who seek to take upon themselves this very great responsibility are enjoined first to be received as deacons and ordained as priests or priestesses, to pass through the training preparatory to the order of bishop, and to consider well the solemnity of the order to which they aspire, before they may be consecrated as bishops among us.

Let any priest or priestess present who is prepared to receive consecration as a bishop, and now wishes to do so, advance to the south of the altar.

(The candidate does so.)

Principal Consecrator: As a priest (or priestess) of the Gnostic Celtic Church, you have followed a path of responsibility and service under the guidance of your own Awen. While you were upon that path no other person could claim the right to pass judgment upon your priestly office and work. A bishop of our church, however, bears certain responsibilities that pass beyond those incumbent on priests and priestesses. As a bishop you will embody the whole tradition of the Gnostic Celtic Church and of the Ancient Order of Druids in America, so that you may communicate these to others according to their readiness to learn and labor.

The duties you are about to assume thus extend not only to yourself, but also to the Gnostic Celtic Church and the Ancient Order of Druids in America, and to every member of these bodies, from the highest to the lowest grade. It is therefore fitting, before you take this step, that you seek the approval both of the Grand Grove and of the members of the order here assembled. The permission of the Grand Grove you have already received.

I therefore ask all those who are present here to consider in your heart this candidate for the order of bishop. If you know of any reason why he (or she) should not advance to this highest station among us, declare it now, but be mindful of your own condition.

(Any person who has anything to say is heard out. If there is no objection, the ceremony continues.)

Principal Consecrator: Then I ask all present to declare with one voice: We bless and affirm this rite of consecration.

All present: We bless and affirm this rite of consecration.

(If more than one bishop assists in the consecration, the questions that follow may be divided among the consecrators.)

Principal Consecrator: It is well. The traditions of our church further require that certain questions be asked and answered of each candidate before the ceremony of ordination can proceed. Have you completed the necessary studies and been initiated as an Adept in the Ancient Order of Druids in America?

(The candidate answers.)

Principal Consecrator *(or other bishop)*: Have you performed the vigil expected of a priest or priestess who seeks advancement to this order, and seriously contemplated the solemnity of the work you propose to undertake?

(The candidate answers.)

Principal Consecrator *(or other bishop)*: Have you properly requested consecration as a bishop from the Grand Grove of the Ancient Order of Druids in America, and passed through the process of training, reflection and conversation that is enjoined on all candidates for the order of bishop?

(The candidate answers.)

Principal Consecrator *(or other bishop)*: Do you now affirm, upon due reflection, your own lifelong commitment to the work and way of the Gnostic Celtic Church and the Ancient Order of Druids in America?

(The candidate answers.)

Principal Consecrator *(or other bishop)*: Are you now prepared, of your own free will, to be consecrated as a bishop in the Gnostic Celtic Church, and to commit yourself to the work of our church and our order from this day onward forever?

(The candidate answers.)

Principal Consecrator *(or other bishop)*: In the name of what deity or sacred power do you take this most serious step?

(The candidate answers.)

Principal Consecrator: It is well. You will therefore kneel on both your knees and silently invoke the blessing of *(name of deity or sacred power)* upon this ceremony and your work as a bishop hereafter. When you are finished, please say aloud, "So mote it be."

(The candidate does so.)

Principal Consecrator: You will now repeat after me. In the presence of, and speak the name of your deity or sacred power—and the holy powers of nature—and of all who witness this rite—I accept the blessing and the burden—of consecration as a bishop—in the Gnostic Celtic Church—now and forever.—I will preserve the rites and teachings—of the Gnostic Celtic Church—and the Ancient Order of Druids in America—and properly communicate them—to those who seek them worthily.—I will receive deacons—ordain priests and priestesses—and consecrate bishops—according to the traditions and customs of our church—and only with the due approval—of the Grand Grove.—I will never debase the authority—of my high office—by employing it—for any unworthy end—but with my whole heart—will always seek the good—of the Gnostic Celtic Church,—the Ancient Order of Druids in America—and its members of every degree—that I and they—may bring light, blessing and healing—to the living earth—and all that lives upon her.

All bishops present: (raise hands in blessing) And in the name of (name of deity or sacred power) and of all the holy powers of nature I consecrate you as a bishop in the Gnostic Celtic Church. (Bishops place right hands upon candidate's head.) Receive now my blessing and that of the Holy Gnosis.

(Bishops pause at this point, as long as seems appropriate, to transmit the blessing, then remove hands.)

Principal Consecrator: When you were ordained as a priest (or priestess) among us, an anointing upon head and hands sealed your reception and formed the living link uniting you to the body and life of the Gnostic Celtic Church. The act of consecration requires that the blessings there conferred be renewed and increased by the same means. You will therefore raise your hands with the palms up, and bow your head.

(Candidate does so. The principal consecrator takes a few drops of oil and, using the right thumb, draws the three rays of light upon each hand, extending from the heel of the palm out to the tips of the thumb, little finger, and middle finger respectively. The consecrator now bids the candidate place his hands together, palm to palm, and binds them with the white cloth.)

(The principal consecrator then takes another few drops of oil and, with the right thumb, draws the three rays of light on the candidate's brow. The consecrator then cleans thumb with a cloth.)

Principal Consecrator: May the light that was before the worlds descend upon you, and guide you ever in the way of Awen. As the three rays of light revealed to Einigen the Giant, the first of all created beings, all the knowledge that ever was and ever will be, so let the blessings of the Holy Gnosis and the teachings of our church and order grant you guidance, wisdom and peace. In the name of (name of deity or sacred power candidate gave earlier) and of all the holy powers, arise and let us celebrate together the mystery of Communion.

(The new priest or priestess is helped to rise and to unbind his or her hands, which may be cleaned if necessary on the white cloth.)

The Communion ceremony is then performed, with the new bishop as the celebrant. A lection suitable for the occasion should be selected by the candidate beforehand, and read at the usual point in the ceremony; the primary consecrator should be the first person after the newly consecrated bishop to partake of the bread and wine, with any other bishops who may have participated in the ceremony partaking immediately thereafter. Once the Communion ceremony is finished, the new bishop may address the Grove, and then the closing ceremony is performed.

The Gnostic Celtic Church

Index

For further information about the Gnostic Celtic Church
and the Ancient Order of Druids in America, please write
to: AODA, PO Box 996, Cumberland MD 21501 or visit
our website at http://www.aoda.org